Praise for *We Pray Freedom*

"Freedom-cum-justice is not a gift that falls from the sky. It is rather a piece of hard, sustained work that must always struggle against the rulers of this age. Such good work requires preparation and readiness through practice. In this rich, suggestive collection, Theoharis and Hribar invite us to liturgical practice for the sake of such emancipation. Their models of liturgical practice open a wide deposit of images, resources, and perspectives that will prosper such good work. We may be most grateful for their imaginative offer in providing this generative resource."

—**Walter Brueggemann**, Old Testament scholar and author, Columbia Theological Seminary

"*We Pray Freedom* reminds us of this truth: People make social movements not only by speaking in the language of the heart but by singing it—and singing it together. Strategy and tactics matter, of course. But as St. Augustine observed, it is one thing to know the good and quite another to love it. It is love for the good that moves us to act upon it. To achieve change, social movements have to create their own power. Music, prayer, and ritual actions speak this language, allowing us to feel solidarity, celebrate commitment, access hope, inspire creativity, and grow courage. When we sing together, we are not only supporting a movement; we are building it. Much of this collective song is rooted in our shared traditions of faith. The leaders and communities featured in *We Pray Freedom* embody this truth, teaching us to build movements through the harmony of our hearts."

—**Marshall Ganz**, Rita E. Hauser Senior Lecturer in Leadership, Organizing, and Civil Society at the Kennedy School of Government at Harvard University

"There is more to the freedom struggle than mass protest and sign-on letters. There is the well-being of the community and the community's connection to God in the midst of the struggle. Each page of *We Pray Freedom* is testimony—evidence of God's connection with and empowerment of real faith communities in times of actual transition, crisis, grief, hope, and triumph. Receive this evidence and its grounding practices as a gift. May it equip your community for the divine freedom struggle."

—**Lisa Sharon Harper**, author of *Fortune* and *The Very Good Gospel*, and president and founder of Freedom Road

"*We Pray Freedom* helps us breathe. During disarray and turmoil, we need prayers, rituals, and words to give forth new life and help sustain and empower us. Editors Liz Theoharis and Charon Hribar give us a beautifully written, uplifting, powerful, and challenging book that will change the way we see worship, community, and the world."

—**Grace Ji-Sun Kim**, professor of theology at Earlham School of Religion and author of *When God Became White* and other books

"*We Pray Freedom* is a powerful testament to the sacred call for justice and liberation, woven together by the voices of grassroots faith and community leaders. Liz Theoharis and Charon Hribar have crafted a living, breathing collection of songs, prayers, and rituals that ignite hope and inspire action. This book is a soul-stirring invitation to embody love in public, a toolkit for those who believe faith must move us toward freedom."

—**Rev. Dr. Jacqui Lewis**, senior minister of Middle Collegiate Church and author of *Fierce Love* and *The Just Love Story Bible*

"*We Pray Freedom* is a call to move beyond the confines of traditional worship into a deeper, more inclusive prayer that embraces both our humanity and our divine calling. It beckons us to hear the cries of the oppressed—not as distant voices, but as teachers of a liberation that transforms us all. The liturgies found in this collection are not just words but powerful acts of justice and compassion that invite us into right relationship with each other, with creation, and with God. This book invites us to deepen our spiritual practice while also answering the call to justice, reminding us that true freedom comes when we walk in solidarity with the marginalized and recognize them as the bearers of sacred truth."

—**Richard Rohr**, Franciscan friar, ecumenical teacher, author, and founder of the Center for Action and Contemplation

"*We Pray Freedom* offers an amazing and inspirational journey through the immense value of the incorporation of rituals and prayers within our multi-diverse communities. The vivid personal stories, the in-depth references to spiritual resources, and the encouragement to 'reflect, embody, discuss' at the end of each chapter gently, yet persistently, guide the reader toward a new vision of possibility. Through each chapter, *We Pray Freedom* offers a powerful blueprint for individuals, churches, unions, and organizations to work together toward liberation, justice, and equality for all. This is our first/next step."

—**Sweet Honey in the Rock**

WE PRAY FREEDOM

WE PRAY FREEDOM

LITURGIES AND RITUALS FROM THE FREEDOM CHURCH OF THE POOR

EDITED BY LIZ THEOHARIS AND CHARON HRIBAR

BROADLEAF BOOKS
Minneapolis

WE PRAY FREEDOM
Liturgies and Rituals from the Freedom Church of the Poor

30 29 28 27 26 25 1 2 3 4 5 6 7 8 9

See the back matter for a full list of contributors and additional permissions information.

Library of Congress Control Number: 2024060959 (print)

Cover design: Broadleaf Books

Print ISBN: 979-8-8898-3034-4
eBook ISBN: 979-8-8898-3035-1

Printed in China.

CONTENTS

www.weprayfreedom.org

We Pray Freedom features a companion website to explore songs, videos, visual art, photos, and other resources that bring the book's rituals to life. As you read, look for this icon 🌐; it signals that there is additional material available online to deepen your experience.

INTRODUCTION

AN ACTIVE, JUSTICE-BUILDING understanding of prayer and ritual motivates our work and this book. Just like the persistent widow in the Gospel of Luke, we are witnesses to and practitioners of embodied prayer. When we pray, we do not simply invoke the yearnings of our hearts through words. We use all of our senses and abilities—our mouths, lungs, ears, minds, hands, and feet—to fight for a world that honors the dignity and sacredness of all life.

In the parable of the persistent widow, Jesus charges his followers to pray without ceasing. But instead of offering a specific prayer or ritual, he tells the story of a poor woman who persistently petitions a powerful judge to grant her and her community justice for wrongs done to them. The judge, who, according to the text, doesn't care about people nor fears God, refuses to hear the widow's pleas. But rather than be discouraged, the woman keeps returning, unyielding in her demand for justice. Eventually, the judge relents, not because he agrees with her demands, but because he is overpowered by her persistence and worries that if he doesn't give in, she might give him a black eye. When the woman finally gets justice, it is because she refused to turn back or back down.

Readers of the Bible and people of faith often deem ritual and prayer as individual, personal, and passive acts of devotion. Within this worldview, poor and dispossessed people like the persistent widow from Luke's Gospel are viewed as victims in need of saving. But Jesus's parable flips this weak and paternalistic common sense on its head. By focusing on this woman, he teaches his followers that the organizing of a poor and dispossessed widow is the highest form of prayer. In this parable, the widow's petitions are not mere words, but a powerful and active ritual asserting the hope that society can be transformed to uplift life, and especially the lives of the oppressed. In the eyes of Jesus, the woman's prayers are a revolutionary lesson that a better and more just world can be created by the very people harmed by injustice.

This parable, like so many in the Bible, resonates today. In 2005, leaders of the Restaurant Opportunities Center (ROC-NY) started holding weekly faith vigils to demand higher wages and better working conditions from Fireman Hospitality Group, a chain of high-end restaurants in New York City known for racial and gender discrimination, stealing tips and wages, and threatening and illegally disciplining their employees. Because these low-wage workers were excluded from labor protections that would allow them to organize in more traditional ways—like holding protests and picket lines—they got creative. Learning that the law stipulates that people have the right to assemble in public to pray together (even though it fails to protect freedom of speech and the right to organize and protest more generally), they decided to hold regular prayer vigils outside Fireman's restaurants.

At the time, we were deeply involved in faith-based, antipoverty organizing across the city. ROC-NY asked our crew of faith and community leaders to help obtain permits for the vigils and pull together the vigil programs, including organizing clergy and seminarians to lead the services. At one of the first prayer vigils, our colleague Jeff Mansfield preached on the parable of the persistent widow. He asserted that these vigils, and the ongoing actions and organizing of restaurant workers, were forms of prayer just like that of the widow. These were rituals that claimed a very simple and radical moral resolution: "Everybody's Got a Right to Live."

Eventually, after mounting public pressure, Fireman relented, and ROC-NY won many of their demands. In the process, they reminded the world that ritual and prayer are not confined to institutional walls or religious doctrine. Just like the persistent widow, the unwavering demands of these low-wage workers were proof that ritual and prayer are deeply rooted in and transformed by the daily struggle for freedom and justice.

PRAYING AS WE PROTEST

Today, many people view ritual and prayer in ways that are formulaic, insular, and individualistic. For people of faith, prayer is often stripped of its dynamic and life-affirming power, while for more secular people, prayer often seems irrelevant or a relic of the past. Across our society, there is a common assumption, whether consciously held or not, that ritual and prayer simply maintain conventional social norms and prop up the status quo.

But for those engaged in struggles for justice, and for the millions of poor and dispossessed people in this country who have been abandoned in this time of great abundance, ritual and prayer remain radical acts of collective sustenance, care, innovation, and transformation. Rituals, prayers, and *liturgies*—translated from the Greek as the "work of the people"—help build right relationships with God and contribute to a vision of society where everyone can thrive. By putting the moral, political, and epistemological agency of the poor at the center, these practices become essential tools for advancing social change.

Rituals and prayers that emerge from the struggle for justice reflect who we are and what we believe in, both individually and collectively. They mark different milestones in our lives and in the lives of social movements. They reinforce a sense of identity and lift up the histories of our communities. They honor grassroots leaders and unsung saints, and they claim legitimacy and authority for people who have been treated as disposable their entire lives. They also serve as tools for political education, waking us up to the reality that social change is possible and helping to build the confidence and leadership of poor and dispossessed people. Rituals remind us that we are the ones we've been looking for!

Although the heart of all our sacred texts and religious traditions emphasize the prayerful leadership of those who have been looked over, left out, and locked up, poor and dispossessed communities are too often excluded from mainstream rituals and denied access to practices that help mark significant occasions. Key rights, such as death and proper burial, are often denied to the poor, who are told that their cultures and traditions are damaged, debased, or disgraceful. Poor people also often lack the money and ability to "pay to play" within today's cultural and religious institutions, leaving them further alienated from these vital practices.

At the same time, the rituals of empire, which reinforce the structures of power and oppression, can be found everywhere. Rituals of war include automatically registering thousands of young people with the Selective Service even as people are denied automatic registration for voting and democratic participation. Rituals of religious nationalism include insisting young people pledge allegiance to the flag and God in schools that are being resegregated, curtailing LGBTQIA2S+ rights, and failing to adequately provide books, history, music, and art. And rituals of idolatry regularly valorize politicians and corporate leaders who, in the words of Rev. Dr. William Barber II, both *pray* and *prey* on the poor.

We must deconstruct and disrupt these rituals of empire and reclaim and reframe traditions that affirm life and the ability for all of us to thrive.

THE FREEDOM CHURCH OF THE POOR

This book of rituals and prayers emerges from grassroots organizing and social movements led by the poor to end poverty and its interlocking injustices. The liturgies of liberation found in these pages are offered by everyday people, community organizers, pastors, and scholars committed to the abolition of poverty. They emerge from work that spans the past two decades and inspired the launch of the Freedom Church of the Poor (FCOP) in 2020.

FCOP is a loose network of workers, poor folks, pastors, organizers, thinkers, and fighters who are bound together by the conviction that things don't have to be this way and that this is not as good as it gets. In FCOP, we believe that God's promise of abundance means an end to poverty and the systemic injustices of our society. Organized by the

Kairos Center, one of the anchor organizations of the Poor People's Campaign: A National Call for Moral Revival, and one of the convenors of the All of Us Initiative, which brings faith and secular leaders together to build a pro-democracy society, FCOP draws on a long tradition of freedom churches that have rejected the religion of empire. By championing a life-affirming theology, it counters a death-dealing theology that blames the poor for their poverty, pits poor and dispossessed people against each other, and promotes the false narrative that poverty cannot be ended but only alleviated through charity.

FCOP gets its name from a speech Rev. Dr. Martin Luther King Jr. gave in the lead-up to the 1968 Poor People's Campaign. During his Massey Lecture series on Canadian public radio in 1967, King called for a massive organizing drive of poor and dispossessed people and explained that if the poor could organize and unite across their differences, they would become a "new and unsettling force in our complacent national life." This force, according to Dr. King, would be a multiracial and interreligious "non-violent army of the poor" and a "freedom church of the poor."

Here, Dr. King was likely drawing on the legacy of the African Methodist Episcopal Zion Church (AME), which, since the days of abolition, has been an enduring home to prophetic faith and social activism and is colloquially known as the "Freedom Church." Although the AME church offered a strong base of support for King, he was not wholly nor specifically referring to the institutional church when he invoked the idea of the freedom church of the poor. Very few Christian denominations endorsed the 1968 Poor People's Campaign, and he challenged organized religion, as a whole, to see how it was failing to do God's work of justice and called on it to live into the Freedom Church tradition.

Today, FCOP draws on the history of struggle by poor and dispossessed people who have consistently lifted up God's vision of justice, freedom, and an abundant life for all. It acknowledges that the Bible is overflowing with prophets and leaders who faced oppressive conditions under the rule of empire, similar to us today. And it argues that our scriptural teachings are not abstract moral lessons but concrete guides for how to organize a multiracial movement of the poor and dispossessed.

Throughout American history, it is the struggles of the poor that have preserved and advanced these lessons. The litany of powerful and prophetic movements is long: the abolitionist movement, the Southern Tenant Farmers Union, the Black freedom struggle, the Poor People's Campaign of 1968, the National Welfare Rights Union, the National Union of the Homeless, and countless others. These multiracial movements sought to unite diverse sections of the poor and dispossessed and called for a fundamental transformation of our society. They weren't organized through institutional religion, but like all movements of the poor, they reimagined the moral values of our society and unapologetically brought revolutionary rituals and prayers directly into the public square. These movements are also part of the Freedom Church tradition.

When the Kairos Center launched FCOP just weeks into the COVID-19 pandemic, we wrote,

> We believe in the fundamental dignity and value of all life and in a world of abundance where all can thrive. We gather as a community of faith to support and care for each other. We commit to realizing the abundant world God promises by identifying, developing, and uniting leaders who will build a movement to end poverty led by the poor. In this community and through our commitment to this struggle we also seek to rediscover and share a vision and practice of religion that is rooted in truth, justice, and love.

More than a place to gather on Sundays, FCOP has become a spiritual and political home for hundreds of poor and dispossessed people that brings together and reflects interfaith, interspiritual, and nonreligious struggles for justice from every region of the country. FCOP nurtures a moral leadership that is committed to ending poverty, systemic racism, ecological devastation, militarism, and the false narrative of Christian nationalism. At FCOP, we define *ritual* as a purposeful and symbolic practice that emerges from, evokes, and nurtures profound layers of feeling and thought. Grounded in the lived experiences of our members—encompassing our stories, needs, moral authority, and desires—our rituals and prayers embody the values and intentions of our communities. They serve to deepen and mend relationships among our people and in the broader world. Our liturgies of liberation bear witness to the hope and love we have for poor and dispossessed people and our faith that transformative change is both necessary and possible.

HOW TO USE THIS BOOK

We Pray Freedom does not follow a traditional liturgical calendar year, in which rites and prayers are dictated from the top down and only certain places and moments in time are considered sacred. Rather, the form and structure of this book arise out of the experience of prayer and collective action by those at the bottom of society who are building the Freedom Church of the Poor. These rituals and prayers provide a small window into this movement. We hope you will not just read them but use them in your own individual and collective lives. We hope you will adapt them to your context and recognize and honor the powerful communities from which they emerge.

These rituals and prayers are, in part, a way to correct the false moral narrative which suggests the poor are responsible for their poverty. They are one of the many keys needed to unlock and undo interlocking injustices that maintain poverty's strong grip on our society. Indeed, the rituals and prayers found in this book assert that the poor and dispossessed are beloved of God, and that God can be discovered in our daily struggles for survival and justice. Much like the biblical Psalms, these rituals and prayers allow us to believe in and move toward the realization of God's kingdom here on earth.

We Pray Freedom explores the profound and multifaceted role that ritual, prayer, and cultural offerings play in a broken world yearning for collective restoration. Grounded in the rich principles and lives of those who participate in the Freedom Church of the Poor tradition, it guides you through a journey of reflection, action, and celebration. Drawing inspiration from Dr. King's belief that "the arc of the moral universe is long, but it bends toward justice," we acknowledge the enduring struggle for social transformation and the need to find more and better ways to sustain ourselves and our communities throughout this lifelong journey.

The chapters of this book explore the intersecting needs for collective remembering (chapter 1), healing (chapter 2), mourning (chapter 3), action (chapter 4), and celebration (chapter 5) within our communities. These first five chapters delve into stories of resistance and struggle that have fostered and been held up by liturgies of the poor and dispossessed. Each of these chapters begins with a brief commentary that we (Liz and Charon) wrote, offering perspectives on various faith practices and cultural offerings that support movements for social change. Following these introductions, we spotlight rituals, prayers, poetry, and songs created and used by social movements in the midst of struggle.

The final chapter (chapter 6) offers a curated collection of additional prayers, rituals, and cultural offerings. This chapter serves as a wellspring of inspiration and practical resources for readers seeking to embrace the spirit of the Freedom Church of the Poor as a catalyst for change. With diverse offerings that address interconnected issues of injustice, it encapsulates the essence of a community mobilized by a shared commitment to transforming the world.

In addition to this book itself, we offer a companion website that includes songs, videos, visual art, photos, and other resources that further bring the rituals in this book to life. You can find these resources at **www.weprayfreedom.org**. Throughout the pages of this book, look for this icon, which indicates additional material that can be found on the website: 🌐

We encourage you to share this book and website with communities and congregations seeking to build a world of peace, justice, and freedom. You are free to use and adapt the resources in this book and on the website to your own context and the community you inhabit. We'd simply ask that you give credit to this book as the source, and that you honor the community from which the liturgy emerged. When using a particular ritual in public, you may want to read an excerpt from the story that appears before the ritual (or from the headnote for the resource) as a way to ground the ritual in the community that created it. We encourage you to find ways to keep these rituals connected to rather than extracted from their contexts. Doing so honors the work and integrity of the community from which a particular liturgy emerged and connects your own community to the larger web of struggle and solidarity.

In 1964, on a trip to Arizona State, Rev. Dr. Martin Luther King Jr. made it clear that only concerted action ever solved or would solve the nation's problems. Much like the persistent widow in Luke's Gospel, Dr. King challenged the idea of patience—of hoping and passively praying our way to justice. "Don't get me wrong. Prayer has been one of the great resources in my own life," he said. "But I am saying that God never intended for prayer to be a substitute for work and intelligence."

We offer the rituals and prayers in this book as our way of honoring and expanding on this basic truth as articulated by Dr. King. They represent liturgies of the people: the work and intelligence of leaders who have been told by society that they are lazy, crazy, and stupid. Through these rituals and prayers, thousands of ordinary but extraordinary people are building a Freedom Church of the Poor that is becoming a new and unsettling force in our complacent national life. Through their inextricable marriage of prayer and moral action, they are lifting from the bottom of our soul-sick society, so that one day everybody might rise together.

CHAPTER ONE

REMEMBRANCE

TRADITIONS THAT BIND us to our ancestors can guide us through current challenges and inspire us to work toward building a new world. These traditions, developed and nurtured by communities in struggle, hold immense strength. However, when removed from their historical contexts and practiced in isolation, their true intention and value can become obscured.

The Freedom Church of the Poor tradition seeks to ground our practices in the struggles and wisdom of those who came before us. It urges us to remember, reflect, and reclaim. As we embark on a pilgrimage of remembrance, we step into the footprints of communities that have sustained and empowered themselves through rituals across the ages. We explore the origins of contemporary rituals of remembrance, reflecting on whose needs they once served and how they are being reimagined by today's struggles for justice.

Rituals of remembrance bridge social movements across generations. They remind us that social change is not a fleeting spark but a slow-burning flame, tended by generations of dedicated leaders. The struggle for justice is neither easy nor swift, but within the history of struggle we discover stories of courage and resilience that fuel our hope and determination. Remembrance is not a passive act; it is a commitment to the belief that change is not only possible but necessary. Rituals of remembrance make this commitment tangible and affirm the truth that we are not alone. The perseverance, strength, and vision of our ancestors fortify our dedication to fight for a better and more just world today. The legendary social activist and song leader Bernice Johnson Reagon once said, "I do remember, that's why I believe." 🌐

When rituals of remembrance are grounded in the experience of movement building and collective struggle, they become kindling for action, illuminating our quest to transform the world. As the prophet Amos proclaims, God desires justice over empty rituals. Micah echoes this sentiment, urging us to act justly, love mercy, and walk humbly (see Amos 5:21–24 and Micah 6:6–8). Through our own justice-seeking rituals, we walk with our ancestors, acknowledging their struggles and carrying their torch forward. We recognize that our fight is not for individual freedom but for the liberation of all.

Today, narratives of struggle are often distorted or silenced by those in power. History is too often told from the perspective of the victors, leaving the voices of those on the bottom unheard. Rituals of remembrance play a vital role in lifting up the untold stories and memories of those who fought and died for social change. They remind us that we must take collective responsibility for bringing about a world where all life can thrive.

In this chapter, we learn about several rituals of remembrance.

Passover Seder: The Passover Seder, celebrated by Jewish people around the world, is a foundational reminder that God is a God of liberation who responds to the cries of the poor and oppressed. The Freedom Shul of the Poor, in collaboration with the Freedom Church of the Poor, hosts annual Seders, using this traditional ritual to reflect on and connect with current struggles for justice. By evoking the freedom struggles of our ancestors, we help a new generation of leaders understand and remember the significance of our history and the responsibility we have to keep that history alive in our own freedom struggles today. Through this act of remembrance, we recommit to building a just society.

Communion: In the Freedom Church of the Poor tradition, Communion is both a reflection and a call to action, compelling us to ask, Who is at the table? Rooted in the struggles of the poor and dispossessed, this sacred practice recalls that the first Communion was held in Bethany, "the house of the poor," and this chapter recounts Rev. Tonny Algood's Easter Sunday celebration with individuals in a homeless encampment in Mobile, Alabama. This story highlights the importance of the place and people with whom we celebrate Communion. It serves as a reminder that God consistently chooses the poor and challenges the rich, emphasizing the sharing of bread and the inclusivity of our gatherings. At the Freedom Church of the Poor, Communion affirms the dignity of all people, reclaiming the ritual as a testament to the sanctity of every life.

Stations of the Cross: This ritual, observed by some Christian communities on Good Friday, reenacts Jesus's journey to the cross. Chaplains on the Harbor, a group that is part of the Freedom Church of the Poor in Washington state, has adapted the stations of the cross to address contemporary social issues. Their practice is rooted in God's preferential option for the poor, reminding us of the divine solidarity that exists between God and those suffering from injustice in a world of abundance. Indeed, throughout the Bible and in our own lives, God is aligned with the oppressed and calls for a radical commitment to justice and compassion.

Día de los Muertos and All Saints' Day: These rituals of remembrance engage every fiber of our being, bridging the boundary between the living and the dead. Such rituals are forms of resistance in a death-dealing society that devalues human life and treats poor and dispossessed people as disposable. Through these sacred practices, we recognize the interconnectedness of our struggle for justice and commit to carrying forward the struggles of those who have come before us. In this section we learn from rituals of remembrance created by the Freedom Church of the Poor, La Iglesia del Pueblo, and La Union de Vecinos in Los Angeles, and are reminded of the enduring beauty, strength, and power of our ancestors. When we come together as a community to remember, we become fully alive—we are emboldened by the legacy of our ancestors as we march into the future with eyes full of hope.

Longest Night of the Year: This ritual, observed on the winter solstice, calls upon our shared responsibility to care for the often forgotten and cast out members of our communities. It reminds us how to honor those who have lost their lives to the harsh realities of our world and the systemic injustices that perpetuate them. In December

2019, the Lancaster County Homeless Union in Pennsylvania provided a community space to share stories of loved ones lost to homelessness, poverty, and systemic injustice. Homelessness remains a national emergency in the United States, with millions facing precarious living conditions and growing criminalization. In life and in death, we refuse to allow our communities to go unnoticed. By reimagining and reclaiming this ritual, we step into a long tradition of liberatory resistance by poor and dispossessed people.

As we embark on this journey of remembrance, let us honor the sacrifices of our ancestors and rekindle the flames of justice they once ignited. When we remember, we reclaim not only our past but also our future.

PASSOVER SEDER: THE STORY

The Passover (Pesach) Seder, a cornerstone of Jewish tradition, celebrates the liberation of the ancient Israelites from slavery and oppression under the Egyptian Empire. The story of Exodus, recounted annually during the Seder, is the story of a people who emerged at the margins, in a marginal land, among marginal people struggling to organize society in a new way. As the Israelites began to organize and demand their freedom, the story reminds us that a "mixed multitude" rallied alongside them: a diverse group of poor, exploited, and suffering people who came together to fight for freedom. And as they did, this narrative underscores a profound message: God is a God of liberation, and divine power is manifest when communities come together to fight for justice.

Passover is not merely a commemoration of the Israelites' escape from Egypt. It is a didactic event that teaches future generations about the divine intervention that brought them out of Egypt; the courage, leadership, and determination required to overthrow unjust orders; and the responsibilities that liberation entails. The Tanak and the Talmud both reinforce this remembrance as an act of recommitment to building a just society. The story of Exodus serves as a continuous reminder of

God's presence in history, responding to the cries of the oppressed and intervening with transformative power.

This powerful story continues to inspire and guide those organizing for justice. In the mid-2000s, organizers like Kate Kanelstein and Sarah Weintraub integrated the Passover Seder into their organizing efforts with the Vermont Workers' Center. Kate explained that while she had grown up in a Jewish family going to and hosting Seders, this tradition had not been meaningful to her as a child. However, as she became more politically active, particularly in campaigns for living wages and against student debt, the Passover story and Seder rituals took on new meaning.

As Kate got involved with the Vermont Workers' Center and their Healthcare Is a Human Right campaign, she, Sarah, and others began hosting annual Seders before major May Day mobilizations, inviting campaign participants to join. The Seder became a way to ground their community, fostering deep relationships and a shared commitment to justice. Sarah explained that they didn't change much about the Seder rituals themselves; rather, they used the familiar symbols and practices to teach about leadership, struggle, and what we're up against—underscoring that the powers that be will not simply "let our people go."

One example is the practice of washing each other's hands at the beginning of the Seder, symbolizing care and trust. Performing this ritual with a community of poor and dispossessed leaders in Vermont helped build deep relationships as they fought for health care. The Seder became a space to share stories, engage in care practices, and strengthen their collective resolve.

Sarah also reflected on the Seder's symbols, which embody the reality of struggle: the burdens and bitterness of exploitation, the terror of struggle and escape, and the joy of liberation. These rituals compel participants to recognize these same conditions and possibilities for redemption in their own time. The story of Exodus, though ancient, is told today to remind us that the fight for liberation is ongoing. "Escaping and fighting for our liberation is *the* story of who we are," Sarah explained. "You must know this in your body, in your heart, in your mind, in your mouth, in your everything—you must experience this and teach this to your children." It is a reminder that liberation is not done. We must continue this fight.

In 2020, as the COVID-19 pandemic began, a group of Jewish leaders involved in the movement to end poverty held a virtual Seder with movement leaders across the country. As they tried to make sense of what was happening in the world and how they were going to continue to organize together, this proved to be an important moment. The 2020 Seder birthed a core group of organizers that today make up the Freedom Shul of the Poor.

Rebecca Schuchat, another movement leader who has helped to develop the Freedom Shul Haggadah, explained that the Seder offers an important blueprint for organizing today. It is a ritual, a meal, and a vehicle for discussion, bringing together newcomers and seasoned leaders alike. The Seder serves as an ancient tool for political education and organizing, teaching that the fight for justice is ongoing and collective.

The commandment to retell the story annually is more than tradition; it's a mandate to bring new voices into the fold, ensuring that the flames of resistance continue to burn brightly. The Seder unites organizers, movement leaders, and families to recount their ancestors' escape from bondage and draw lessons for today. During the Seder, participants study the steps taken by the enslaved Israelites to break the power of Pharaoh and cross the Red Sea, and wrestle with what it will take to blaze our own path toward freedom. Participants immerse themselves in the sacred rituals and the songs and dig deep into this foundational story of revolution by poor and dispossessed people. They praise the God of liberation, the divine presence awakened in the struggles of the oppressed to be free.

The Passover Seder has become an important space for movement leaders across faith backgrounds. Its profound impact lies in its ability to connect ancient narratives of liberation with contemporary struggles for justice. It is a reminder that liberation is an ongoing process, requiring continual effort and commitment. As Sarah Weintraub says, building a movement is not just a task but a way of life, integrating spiritual, political, and cultural practices. The Seder, therefore, is more than a ritual; it is a call to action, a blueprint for resistance, and a commitment to carry forward the struggle for liberation. The Freedom Shul of the Poor Haggadah introduction captures this sentiment:

> We affirm our commitment, alongside countless others, to write the next chapter of Exodus, not on the page, but out there, in the world. We draw deep inspiration from this ancient story which, at its heart, is about the power that is always possible when the poor and dispossessed unite across manufactured lines of division and fortified borders. Indeed, the Torah teaches that it is not just the Israelites who escape the bondage of Pharaoh. Alongside them are the *Erev Rav*, a mixed multitude of other enslaved people who cross the Red Sea together.

This ancient story of liberation reminds us that throwing off the shackles of oppression is not just possible; it is necessary. The Seder's enduring power reminds us that when the poor and dispossessed unite across lines of division, true liberation is within reach.

PASSOVER SEDER: THE RITUAL

Included here are excerpts from the Freedom Shul of the Poor 2024 Passover Seder. The full 2024 Freedom Shul of the Poor Haggadah can be found online. 🌐

MAGGID PART IV (TELLING OF THE PASSOVER STORY—PARTING THE RED SEA)

This midrash tells the story of leadership—the leadership of poor and dispossessed people like Nachshon, who have nothing to lose and take life-saving action from a place of necessity. In this time of crisis, leaders like

Nachshon become clear, recognizing that behind them is only death, and in front of them the hope of freedom.

Reader 1: Let's return to the last part of the story. Our mixed multitude made its way to the sea, to the great gap that exists between slavery and freedom. And, just as everyone knew would happen, Pharaoh changed his mind one last time. He set out in armed pursuit to bring them back into servitude. And so they found themselves trapped, Pharaoh's army behind them and this impossibly large body of water ahead. They cried out to God in fear, and they confronted Moses, saying, "Was it for want of graves in *Mitzrayim* that you brought us to die in the wilderness?" They told Moses that they knew they should never have left. While bondage was bad, death in the wilderness was worse.

Reader 2: Moses replied, telling the Israelites not to be afraid and that God would fight for them and free them from slavery forever. And God told Moses, "Why do you cry out to me? Tell the Israelites to go forward." This freedom struggle had all begun when the Israelites cried out and God heard them, but now the struggle was in a new stage. This was a time for action, and the people had to move bravely forward together to free themselves. There was no going back to the broken "normal" of life under Pharaoh.

Reader 1: Some versions of this story teach that in this decisive moment, the Israelites didn't listen, and the tribes fell to fighting among themselves. At the critical moment, their hard-won unity began to break apart. In the midst of all this arguing and fear, a man named Nachshon ran forward and leapt into the sea. He advanced deeper and deeper, the water rising past his mouth and up to his nostrils. Only then, with not even an inch to breathe, did God instruct Moses how to split the sea.

Reader 2: And as the sea split, and a path opened up from narrowness and toward the abundance that God promises, the people moved forward together. Behind them, God took the wheels off of Pharaoh's chariots and the army of the empire was thrown into confusion and disorganization and finally swallowed up by the sea.

At the most important moment—which was also the most chaotic and uncertain time—what decided the outcome of this great fight was which side was able to stay organized. The mixed multitude of poor and oppressed people stuck together, while Pharaoh's army fell apart. These people—our ancestors—made it to the other side of the sea.

By coming together, they had thrown off an empire. They had arrived on the shores of freedom.

WELCOMING ELIJAH

This next section of the Haggadah was written for the 2023 Freedom Shul of the Poor Seder by Daniel Jones (University of the Poor and Freedom Shul of the Poor) and adapted by Harrison Farina (Put People First! PA [PPF-PA]) for the 2024 Passover Seder. This reading lifts up a critical struggle against the criminalization of homelessness in the United States. You could adapt this to your context by replacing the last portion of Reader 2's words with a description of an issue in your community.

Reader 1: As we approach the end of the Seder, we invite the Prophet Elijah to sit at our Seder table. We open the doors to our homes and pour an extra cup of wine or juice for the prophet in the sincere hope that he'll join us. Traditionally, it's said that Elijah is a messenger for the coming of the Messiah, who will arrive to turn the world upside down and right side up—to fulfill all of God's promises of justice, community, and abundant life.

Reader 2: It's worth taking a moment to remind ourselves who Elijah was. He wasn't simply a pious messenger of God. He was a peasant revolutionary who stood up to the wicked rule of an ancient king and exposed the rampant injustice that threatened to destroy his people. He was a leader who understood that his society needed to undergo a radical revolution of values.

Reader 1: When we understand the Prophet Elijah for who he was, we see the coming of the Messiah in an entirely new light. Every year, we open our doors and hope Elijah will be there to announce an ending and a new beginning. But every year we discover that he hasn't come just yet. Not until we're ready. Not until we've followed Elijah's example and taken the steps that lead to freedom. Not until we've cried out, gotten organized, and moved forward together.

Reader 2: There's an old story about Elijah, first written down in the Talmud about fifteen hundred years ago. It's said that a great Rabbi found Elijah and asked him, "When will the Messiah come?" Elijah said, "Go ask him yourself." He told the Rabbi that the Messiah was among the poor lepers outside the gates of Rome and that he could be recognized because while the other lepers untied their bandages all at once, he untied his bandages one at a time, because he wanted to be ready to bring redemption at any moment.

Reader 1: The Rabbi went to the Roman gates and asked the Messiah when the end of evil and the beginning of justice would come. The Messiah replied, "Today." So all day the Rabbi waited, and nothing happened. Eventually, he went back to Elijah and lamented, "The Messiah lied to me! He said that he would come today, but he did not come." Elijah shook his head and corrected the Rabbi: "No. He said he will come today, if only you will listen to his voice." A revolutionary transformation of our society is not something we patiently wait for, but something we usher in by taking action together, guided by the leadership of those who have their backs against the wall, with no choice but to push.

Reader 2: Tomorrow, the Supreme Court will hear the case of Grants Pass v. Johnson, which is the most significant case about homelessness in over forty years. The case will determine whether, under our Constitution, a local government can make it a crime to involuntarily live outside and unsheltered when adequate shelter is not available.

The National Union of the Homeless will be in Washington, DC, to oppose the cruel and unusual punishment of unhoused people. This case represents a bipartisan attack on our communities, with both Republicans and Democrats in support. Municipalities talk about homelessness as a "public health crisis" and claim that we need to "clean up the streets." But who are they really concerned about, and who are they casting aside?

Reader 1: If the state of Rome had laws to "clean up the streets," they would be arresting the Messiah, who sat outside their gates! Today, the Messiah sits among the wounded, hungry, and dispossessed of Gaza and the United States and all over the world, who demand that the world hear their voices.

Go and open our door and invite Elijah in.

[Read the following after the door is opened.]

Take a second to feel the pain of Elijah's absence. Tonight, amid the many hard questions we ask during the Seder, we ask ourselves: why hasn't Elijah arrived? How is it that we aren't ready? What do we do now? How will we bring closer the day when Elijah, and the countless other prophets who have paved a path toward freedom, will see their work realized and join us in celebration?

WE GET THERE TOGETHER: A SONG

This song, written by Joshua Blaine, a Jewish song leader and cultural organizer with Jewish Voice for Peace, was one of many songs lifted up during the Seder. Josh wrote this song in 2022 as part of a We Cry Justice *artists collective project and was inspired by Daniel Jones's chapter from* We Cry Justice, *"A Mixed Multitude." He also drew from the poem by Aurora Levins Morales, "Red Sea," in which she challenges us to ask, What happens this time if we all cross together? We Get There Together has become an important song sung in protest spaces and gatherings calling for a ceasefire in Gaza and more.* 🌐

No one is getting left behind this time
No one is getting left behind
No one is getting left behind this time

We get there together or never get there at all
We get there together or never get there at all
We get there together or never get there at all

REFLECT, EMBODY, DISCUSS

1. How can traditional rituals like the Seder be used as tools for political education and organizing in modern movements? What lessons can be drawn from the Freedom Shul of the Poor's use of the Seder in their efforts to fight for social justice?
2. What do we learn from the story of Nachshon about leadership?
3. What does the story of Elijah and the messiah teach about the role of individual and collective action in achieving social transformation?
4. Reflecting on Joshua Blaine's song "We Get There Together," ask yourself, What "mixed multitude" am I grateful for? What "mixed multitude" do I hope for? What will it mean for us to all "get there together"?

COMMUNION: THE STORY

In August 2005, Hurricane Katrina devastated the Gulf Coast, particularly Louisiana, Mississippi, and Alabama. As one of the worst natural disasters in US history, it resulted in fourteen hundred deaths and displaced up to 1.5 million people. Among those displaced were women from the only shelter for women in southwest Alabama, which was destroyed by the storm. Rev. Tonny Algood, a lifelong organizer and leader in the Freedom Church of the Poor, was then the executive director of the United Methodist Inner City Mission in Mobile, Alabama. He offered the mission as temporary housing for these women when a special city task force could find no other shelter.

In March 2007, McKemie Place opened its doors as an emergency shelter after a homeless woman froze to death on the streets of downtown Mobile. Reflecting on her unnecessary death, Rev. Tonny emphasized that she was "somebody's daughter, or somebody's mother, somebody's sister, or aunt. But most of all, she was a child of God that did not get taken in."

When McKemie Place first opened, its mission was to provide a safe and peaceful place for women, offering hot showers, meals, and services to help them eventually secure housing. The women who stayed there had faced numerous life challenges, leading to hurt, anger, and a volatile atmosphere. Many had low self-esteem and were dealing with tremendous trauma.

Confronting these challenges day in and day out, Rev. Tonny came to realize that the main goal for creating and holding space at McKemie Place was not just to serve the women but to provide them with unconditional love, as God loves us. This shift in perspective transformed the atmosphere at McKemie Place, turning it into a place where all who gathered could experience the spirit of love and the spirit of community. As patrons and staff grew to realize that they were all in the struggle together—that they really needed each other—they came to live into the unconditional love God has for us, enabling them to share that unconditional love with one another.

As the shelter at McKemie Place evolved from a direct service organization into a ministry, Rev. Tonny was granted permission by his district to offer Communion to the women on Good Friday. This Communion service became a cherished tradition, reminding the community that in its origin, the ritual of Communion was a way to show how much we must love and care for each other, especially when we live in a system that believes more in oppression than redemption and salvation.

The significance of this Communion ritual was illuminated one Easter week when one of the former shelter patrons, Stella, called Rev. Tonny just to see how he was doing. Stella was a fiery patron of the shelter. Stella had been through a lot in life, and when she first came to the shelter, she put on a very mean persona—something she needed in order to survive years of living on the streets. Her rough demeanor often led to confrontations with other women at the shelter. But as time went on, this persona softened as Stella got to know and love the community at McKemie Place. Stella became more and more part of the community.

She would use an old car she acquired to take other women at the shelter to the store to do their shopping.

Now living in a homeless encampment with her boyfriend Billy, Stella expressed how much she wished she could have been at the shelter that Good Friday to take Communion, as she hadn't received it in a long time. Rev. Tonny offered to come to the encampment on Easter Sunday and serve Communion there. So, on Easter Sunday, Rev. Tonny and his wife brought the sacraments to the encampment, setting up a simple altar with a white tablecloth, a cross, bread, and grape juice. Among the small group gathered was a young man who expressed his gratitude for receiving Communion, noting he hadn't been able to attend church because he had no suitable clothes.

As they began the Communion ritual, Rev. Tonny noticed that Billy didn't fully understand what it was about, so he paused to explain: "Jesus came to forgive us for our sins if we'd only follow the way—to love God and to love each other. And Jesus did this for everybody."

Billy, who had low self-esteem and struggled with alcoholism, responded, "He didn't do it for me." He had internalized the harmful belief that poor people were sinners and unworthy of receiving sacraments. Rev. Tonny reassured him, "Most certainly Jesus did this for you as much as anyone else in this world." At that moment, Billy realized he was accepted and loved just as he was. Overcome with emotion, he broke down and cried on Rev. Tonny's shoulder before they finished the Communion ritual.

Celebrating the liturgy of Holy Communion in this place, with these people—God's people—was an embodiment of moral resurrection that Easter Sunday. The ritual affirmed that God's presence is strongest in spaces where people come together as a community, recognizing their need for one another. This is the Beloved Community and the true meaning of Communion. Our task in "doing this in remembrance of me" is to ensure that God's will is done on earth as it is in heaven. By celebrating Communion among the poor and dispossessed, we proclaim that poor people aren't sinners, but poverty itself is a sin and God's vision for earth is a world without poverty or opulence.

COMMUNION: THE RITUAL

This ritual is an excerpt from a traditional United Methodist liturgy of Holy Communion, as found in The United Methodist Hymnal. *The full liturgy was celebrated by the Rev. Tonny Algood at a homeless encampment in Mobile. As you read this ritual, consider how Rev. Tonny's story might inspire you to reconnect to the history of rituals practiced in your community and reimagine their practice in new contexts.*

Holy are you, and blessed is your Son Jesus Christ.
Your Spirit anointed him
  to preach good news to the poor,
  to proclaim release to the captives
  and recovering of sight to the blind,
  to set at liberty those who are oppressed,
  and to announce that the time had come
  when you would save your people.
  He healed the sick, fed the hungry, and ate with sinners.
  By the baptism of his suffering, death, and resurrection
  you gave birth to your Church,
  delivered us from slavery to sin and death,
  and made with us a new covenant
  by water and the Spirit.
  When the Lord Jesus ascended,
  he promised to be with us always,
  in the power of your Word and Holy Spirit.

The pastor may hold hands, palms down, over the bread, or touch the bread, or lift the bread.

On the night in which he gave himself up for us,
he took bread, gave thanks to you, broke the bread,
gave it to his disciples, and said:
  "Take, eat; this is my body which is given for you.
  Do this in remembrance of me."

The pastor may hold hands, palms down, over the cup, or touch the cup, or lift the cup.

When the supper was over, he took the cup,
gave thanks to you, gave it to his disciples, and said:
"Drink from this, all of you;
this is my blood of the new covenant,
poured out for you and for many
for the forgiveness of sins.
Do this, as often as you drink it,
in remembrance of me."

The pastor may raise hands.

And so,
in remembrance of these your mighty acts in Jesus Christ,
we offer ourselves in praise and thanksgiving
as a holy and living sacrifice,
in union with Christ's offering for us,
as we proclaim the mystery of faith.

Christ has died; Christ is risen; Christ will come again.

The pastor may hold hands, palms down, over the bread and cup.

Pour out your Holy Spirit on us gathered here,
and on these gifts of bread and wine.
Make them be for us the body and blood of Christ,
that we may be for the world the body of Christ,
redeemed by his blood.

The pastor may raise hands.

By your Spirit make us one with Christ,
one with each other,

and one in ministry to all the world,
until Christ comes in final victory
and we feast at his heavenly banquet.

Through your Son Jesus Christ,
with the Holy Spirit in your holy Church,
all honor and glory is yours, almighty Father,
now and forever.

Amen.

Recite the Our Father (Think about the sharing of bread and the forgiveness of debts).

REFLECT, EMBODY, DISCUSS

1. Has there been a time in your life when you have been excluded, put down, or deemed unworthy? Have you knowingly or unknowingly made another person feel excluded, put down, or unworthy?
2. What actions or encounters called you in—welcomed you to come to the table? What actions can we take to welcome others to the table?
3. How do the locations and communities with which we practice Communion rituals help us reimagine their intention and infuse them with new meaning for our lives today?

STATIONS OF THE CROSS: THE STORY

Grays Harbor County in Washington state, once a thriving timber hub, now faces severe economic decline, with high rates of unemployment, poverty, homelessness, substance use disorders, and inadequate health care. In Aberdeen, more than a thousand of the sixteen thousand residents are homeless, and societal neglect and criminalization are rampant. Poor young adults, in particular, are devalued and criminalized. They are, according to writer and organizer Aaron Scott, "relentlessly scapegoated and pathologized as being wasteful, immoral, licentious and intemperate."

In 2013, Cedar Monroe, a native of Grays Harbor, returned to their hometown after training in street chaplaincy in Boston. They began connecting with people in downtown Aberdeen's back alleys and underpasses, going out with a backpack full of sandwiches. During the time they launched Chaplains on the Harbor, Cedar was in and out of homelessness as well. Gathering a small team of church and street volunteers, Chaplains began to host regular community meals in Aberdeen.

Over the next several years, Chaplains on the Harbor built a ministry to stand with the poor of Grays Harbor County. Through survival projects—daily meals, hygiene supplies, harm reduction, and outreach services—they connected with the community and developed leaders from among those who had experienced homelessness, incarceration, and poverty.

Chaplains on the Harbor is rooted in liberation theology, a belief that God is on the side of the poor. "God takes sides," Cedar reflected. "We as a ministry, and me as a pastor, I take people's side. If a homeless encampment is being evicted, I take their side against the city. If one of my kids is beat up by the police, I take the side of that kid against the police department." This approach is central to the organizing model at Chaplains on the Harbor, where they are building a movement to end poverty, led by those directly impacted by homelessness, incarceration, and addiction.

To build this kind of leadership, people must develop a consciousness that can counter the blame and shame that society places on people for their poverty. To give people space to talk about their real material conditions and to counter the shame imposed on members in their community, Chaplains on the Harbor introduced a ritual practice.

In 2016, a year marked by significant hardship, including numerous deaths and conflicts between encampments and the city, the need for a ritual that could articulate the community's pain and resilience became clear. Chaplains on the Harbor adapted the stations of the cross, a Christian practice that reflects on the last moments of Jesus's life. For centuries, this devotion has been used to meditate on fourteen images that depict

Jesus's suffering and death. Chaplains of the Harbor's version became a way to tell the stories of suffering in their community through Jesus's story.

Inspired by liberation theologian Gustavo Gutiérrez's concept of God's preferential option for the poor, the organizers wrote, "In Grays Harbor, we walk our own Way of the Cross. Jesus lived through all the oppression and suffering of the first-century Roman Empire as he faced arrest and execution. In us, he still suffers as we suffer." For poor and homeless community members in Aberdeen, viewing Jesus as a poor person who led a movement and suffered under the Roman Empire—and connecting that to their own suffering—was a powerful, new perspective.

Participants created stations using pieces of cardboard and photographs depicting local events like campsite raids and police arrests. These images were displayed in the sanctuary, allowing people to walk the stations and see their own stories reflected. The stations of the cross provided a powerful counternarrative to the pathologizing stereotypes about the struggles of poor and unhoused people. The ritual allowed community members to see Jesus as someone who struggled, suffered, and resisted oppression. By reimagining this ritual, they challenged systems that perpetuate poverty and police violence. The ritual empowered individuals to see themselves as valuable and holy and educated others about the harsh realities faced by the poor.

In 2019, amid a lawsuit against the city for threatening homeless sweeps, Chaplains on the Harbor organized another stations of the cross event. They invited the Episcopal bishop (who would be in Aberdeen for Maundy Thursday) and members of the diocese to walk through Aberdeen, stopping at sites of community struggle. At each stop, Chaplains on the Harbor members offered their testimonies about family separation, homelessness, addiction, excessive criminalization, and the unjust, constant early death that plagued their community. This powerful event told a wider story about the material reality in Aberdeen, unearthed the causes of poverty, and called for collective action to end poverty and injustice.

Chaplains on the Harbor organizes for dignity and survival among Jesus's people: the jobless, the homeless, the incarcerated, and the addicted. This practice affirms the dignity of those who are often devalued by society and challenges others to recognize and address the injustices that perpetuate poverty and suffering. Through this reimagining of the stations of the cross ritual, we are able to tell a story of resilience, resistance, and hope, embodying the true spirit of liberation.

By centering the experiences of the poor and dispossessed within the context of Jesus's own story, this ritual empowers and unites people in our communities. Other communities of faith and action have created stations of the cross rituals in their cities and neighborhoods. What might a stations of the cross look like in your community?

STATIONS OF THE CROSS: THE RITUAL

This stations of the cross litany, adapted by Chaplains on the Harbor in Washington state, was held on Maundy Thursday in 2016. It offers a retelling of the stations from the perspective of the poor today. The artworks in this chapter are interpretations of the 2016 stations of the cross created by Katrina Ross Zezza for this project. You can find photographs of the Chaplains on the Harbor ritual on the website. 🌐

Station 1: Jesus Is Condemned to Death
Mark 15:1–5, 15

In Grays Harbor, one of the leading causes of death is drug overdose. After the timber industry crashed, meth manufacturing was one of the replacement industries. Since then, both meth and heroin have been in heavy use to self-medicate for pain, to manage health conditions, and to attempt to survive the brutality of life on the streets. This past year, a young man in our community in Aberdeen, Andrew, died at twenty-three. We are condemned to death, first by economic collapse and then sometimes by our attempts to survive it.

Station 2: Jesus Takes up His Cross
John 19:6, 15–17

In Jesus's time, people who were considered a threat to the empire were executed by crucifixion. As our poverty rates increase, as so many of us end up on the street, as jobs disappear, we so often face our own crosses, while those in power accumulate wealth and leave our communities to die.

Station 3: Jesus Falls the First Time
John 19:1–3

One of the last places to go if you are homeless is Rivercity, the tent city now in Hoquiam. Just like Jesus faced ridicule on the way to the cross, so people there have endured the threats and hatred of the community directed toward them. A giant rock was tossed over into one of the tents one night and could have seriously injured someone.

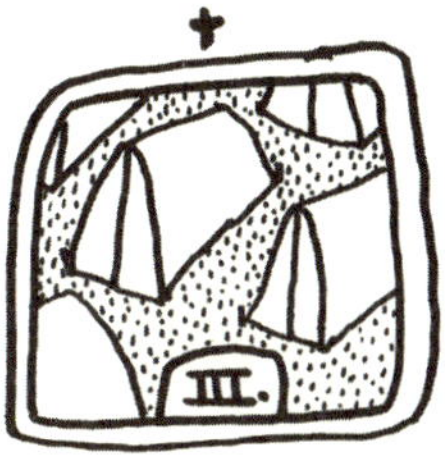

Station 4: Jesus Meets His Sorrowful Mother
John 19: 25–27

Generations of our families have been broken apart. Families are shattered by violence and by a system that robs mothers of their children. Grays Harbor has a high rate of child removal by Child Protective Services from the home and very low rates of family reunification.

Station 5: Simon of Cyrene Helps Jesus Carry the Cross
Mark 15:21

As Jesus, a Palestinian Jew, walks the way of the cross, Simon, a man from North Africa, helps him carry his cross. For the past several months, we have been meeting as the School of Hard Knocks, studying social movements around the country. We aim to build a movement to end poverty, led by the poor, across the lines that divide us.

Station 6: Veronica Wipes the Face of Jesus
Isaiah 53:2–3

In the middle of great suffering, we try to take care of each other. We face police violence, stabbings on the street, and all sorts of violence. In this community, we try to work to heal each other's wounds.

Station 7: Jesus Falls a Second Time
Romans 8:31–39

Those of us who end up homeless often camp out along the Chehalis River. The young man who built this camp spent a great deal of time putting in archways, a small house, and even a stove. When the city evicted the camp in June of last year, his entire structure was bulldozed to the ground.

Station 8: Jesus Meets the Women of Jerusalem
Luke 23:27–31

We are facing times of crisis, and we often fear for our children. The matriarchs in our community help provide mentorship and support.

Station 9: Jesus Falls the Third Time
Psalm 38

We lead the nation in our rates of child incarceration for nonviolent, non-criminal offenses. The school-to-prison pipeline begins very young and continues into adulthood for most of our young people, who cycle frequently in and out of jail. With few legal ways of making money, we participate in an underground economy and are increasingly criminalized.

Station 10: Jesus Is Stripped of His Garments
John 19:23–24

As our young people end up in and out of jail, they are trapped in a cycle of loss. When they are arrested, they usually lose all of their possessions. Constant police harassment and frequent arrests rob us of our dignity, and when released, we have to rebuild all over again.

Station 11: Jesus Is Nailed to the Cross
Luke 23:33–34

So many of us can feel trapped, ever searching for a way out. Those of us who grew up here often want to leave, but there are few places to go. It can feel like we want heaven but keep finding ourselves in hell.

Station 12: Jesus Dies on the Cross
Luke 23:44–46

So many in our community die so young. We have faced many deaths over the past year in our community, and several of them were very young. On All Saints' Day, we named the names of our dead and lit candles to honor their memory.

Station 13: Jesus Is Taken Down from the Cross
John 20:38–42

Too many mothers watch their children die. Stetson, eighteen, was found dead next to his tent a few weeks ago. His mother and sister have been struggling to raise the money to pay for his cremation and funeral. [A collection was taken at this point for Stetson's family.]

Station 14: Jesus Is Laid in the Tomb
Matthew 27:57–60

The artist describes this as a depiction of hovering between life and death and waiting for rebirth. In Grays Harbor, it can feel like hope is a distant dream. It can feel like nothing will ever change. We wonder if redemption is possible.

REFLECT, EMBODY, DISCUSS

1. How do the stories and struggles of the Grays Harbor community resonate with your own experiences or the experiences of people you know?
2. Reflect on the statement that "God takes sides. We as a ministry, and me as a pastor, I take people's side." How does this perspective influence your understanding of justice and advocacy?
3. Have you ever participated in a ritual or ceremony that helped you process or understand injustices? If so, how did it impact you?
4. What stories of struggle would you include in a stations of the cross ritual in your community?

DÍA DE LOS MUERTOS AND ALL SAINTS' DAY: THE STORY

In movements for change, where battles for justice are waged daily, rituals of remembrance emerge as powerful acts of resistance. In a society that often denies the unnecessary deaths caused by violent economic and political systems that justify the death of poor and dispossessed people, reclaiming and practicing these rituals becomes essential for our collective survival. The Freedom Church of the Poor tradition rejects a culture of death and denial, offering communal practices that lift up the memories of fallen fighters and loved ones who have died too soon. These rituals sustain the spirit of those fighting in the present, affirming life and the significance of each individual.

Rituals like Día de los Muertos, which takes place in Mexico and other parts of Latin America, and All Saints' Day are times to remember ancestors, holding them in love and recalling their lives, struggles, and legacies. These practices nourish our interconnectedness and help us continue their fight. The need to reclaim rituals to honor the dead and resist a culture dismissive of unjust deaths was embraced by Freedom Church of the Poor, Iglesia del Pueblo, and Union de Vecinos in Los Angeles, during the COVID-19 pandemic on November 1, 2020.

At a time when over 220,000 people in the United States and more than 1.1 million worldwide had died from COVID-19, and many more from poverty, inequality, and systemic racism, these communities came together to grieve, overcome isolation, and commit to changing unjust systems. They gathered to observe Día de los Muertos and All Saints' Day, celebrating the lives of deceased loved ones and furthering their legacy. As Mother Jones famously said, they gathered to "pray for the dead and fight like hell for the living."

This initial virtual celebration, now an annual event, acknowledged the long history of gathering to remember the deceased. The service highlighted how the New Testament refers to meals of remembrance, like Jesus's Last Supper, which were gatherings of the poor and dispossessed. These acts of remembrance weren't just spiritual; they were also gatherings to remember those who had died at the hands of empire, often too poor to afford a proper burial. These gatherings were projects of survival and mutual aid, harkening back to the Hebrew Bible Exodus story and manna in the wilderness. When Jesus asked his disciples to drink and eat in remembrance of him, it was a ritual to remember the poor—a tradition the early church continued, and the Freedom Church community continues today.

During the service, Kenia Torres-Alcocer of Union de Vecinos constructed a physical altar using digital photos collected from the community. The community also participated in an ancient meal of remembrance, lifting up the memories of those who had died. Leaders proclaimed, "We honor you," and attendees responded, "We do this in your memory." This ritual honored those who taught us to fight for liberation.

Leonardo Vilchis, cofounder and codirector of Union de Vecinos, emphasized that Día de los Muertos is a liminal time when the dead and the living come together, offering the possibility of something new being born. In 2020, amid a global crisis, this time allowed people to recognize that the current state of the world is not how it ought to be. As people awaken to societal contradictions, there is potential for transformation. Leonardo reminded us that this was a time to remember everyone that the system has excluded: the sick, the poor, the working class, the peasant, and the immigrant. This time of remembrance is also a time to commit to building a world where everyone has a life, where everybody has a place, and access to what they need.

Día de los Muertos helps us to honor those who have died and take up the struggle against unjust death today. Charito Calvachi-Mateyko of La Iglesia del Pueblo explains that "Día de los Muertos is a ritual, not just an event. We make this distinction because it means you incorporate your whole being into it. We believe it's a liminal time when the veil between the living and the dead is thinner so we host them in our midst by building an altar or *ofrenda* that includes water to quench the thirst of their journey, their favorite meals, some of their favorite things, toys for children gone too soon, and flowers—usually marigolds, as their strong scent will help guide your ancestors home. Everything's meant to be done with intention as we enter a realm that we don't know anything about; it's bigger than you."

Rituals of remembrance are not just about honoring the dead; they are about healing the living and maintaining a connection across generations. The Freedom Church tradition does not seek to appropriate culturally specific rituals, but in relationship with communities who practice particular rituals, seeks to learn about and incorporate rituals like Día de los Muertos and All Saints' Day into multicultural movements for change. One example is the collective construction of a Día de los Muertos ofrenda or altar. 🌐

Through this practice, we can gain a deeper appreciation of cultural practices that foster a sense of continuity, purpose, and resistance. By collectively reimagining these practices, we are reminded that our fight for justice and equity is part of a larger, ongoing story, one that honors the past, empowers the present, and inspires the future.

As we develop prayers of remembrance and connect with the stories of those who fought for justice, we weave a tapestry of memory and hope that sustains us in our struggles. By embracing these rituals, we honor the legacies of those who came before us and strengthen our resolve to continue their work, ensuring that their memories and values live on through us.

DÍA DE LOS MUERTOS: THE PRAYER

This Prayers of the People was offered during a bilingual Día de los Muertos celebration in New York City in October 2022. Leaders from the Freedom Church of the Poor and La Iglesia del Pueblo gathered with community members at the People's Church in East Harlem. As a hybrid service, leaders from around the United States and several outside countries joined this community virtually to participate in this powerful ritual of remembrance. The Prayers of the People was written by ana g. lara lópez (Kairos Center), Arelis Figueroa (Iglesia del Pueblo), and Charito Calvachi-Mateyko (Iglesia del Pueblo).

We pray for Mother Earth, its rivers that have dried, the melting ice, the ravaging fires, and all natural disasters that reveal our human misdoings.

Response: Oh Sustainer, hear our prayers and lead us into action.

Oramos por la Madre Tierra, sus ríos que se han secado, las capas de hielo que se derriten, los incendios devastadores y todos los desastres naturales que muestran nuestras fechorías humanas.

Respuesta: Oh Sustentador, escucha nuestras plegarias y movilízanos a actuar.

Oramos por las almas de las personas fallecidas en los desiertos, en las montañas, en los ríos y océanos en su camino por una mejor vida. Oramos por sus almas en pena.

Escucha nuestras plegarias y movilízanos a actuar.

We pray for the souls of people who died in deserts, mountains, rivers, and oceans on their way to a better life. We pray for their souls in pain.

Hear our prayers and lead us into action.

We pray for the passing of the Build Back Better plan as it is the least this country can give its people.

Hear our prayers and lead us into action.

Oramos por la aprobación del plan *Build Back Better*, ya que es lo mínimo que este país puede dar a su gente.

Escucha nuestras plegarias y movilízanos a actuar.

Oramos por los niños fallecidos en las montañas a mano del ejército, el gobierno y los sistemas inhumanos en Guatemala y alrededor del mundo. Oímos sus lamentos.

Escucha nuestras plegarias y movilízanos a actuar.

We pray for the children who died in the mountains at the hands of the army, the government, and the inhumane systems in Guatemala and around the world. We hear their wailing.

Hear our prayers and lead us into action.

We pray for the almost five million individuals worldwide who have died in the past year and a half due to COVID-19. Comfort the grieving hearts of their loved ones.

Hear our prayers and lead us into action.

Oramos por los casi 5 millones de personas en todo el mundo que han muerto en el último año y medio debido a COVID-19. Consuela los corazones afligidos de sus seres queridos.

Escucha nuestras plegarias y movilizanos a actuar.

Oramos por cada vida humana a la que se le ha robado la vida debido al racismo. Especialmente a los hombres negros y las mujeres trans negras cuyas vidas son robadas con demasiada frecuencia por sistemas injustos y racistas. Nombramos especialmente a nuestros hermanos en la cárcel de Rikers cuya vida es tomada poco a poco y día tras día.

Escucha nuestras plegarias y movilizanos a actuar.

We pray for every human that has been robbed of a life due to racism, especially Black men and trans Black women whose lives are robbed all too often by unjust, racist systems. We especially hold up our siblings at Rikers, whose lives are taken little by little and day after day.

Hear our prayers and lead us into action.

We pray for the children who have died in detention centers through separation from their parents. We feel the sadness and deep pain of these injustices. We demand immigration reform.

Hear our prayers and lead us into action.

Oramos por los niños que han muerto en centros de detención al haber sido separados de sus padres. Sentimos la tristeza y el dolor profundo de estas injusticias. Demandamos una reforma migratoria.

Escucha nuestras plegarias y movilizanos a actuar.

Oramos por nuestros hermanos/hermanas/hermanes trans, por las personas no-conforme-con-el-género-binario, y miembros de la comunidad LGBTQIA2S+ que hemos perdido. Oramos por sus familias, amigos y por todos los que están en proceso de duelo por su pérdida.

Escucha nuestras plegarias y movilizanos a actuar.

We pray for our trans, gender nonconforming, and LGBTQIA2S+ siblings we've lost, their families, friends, and all who grieve them.

Hear our prayers and lead us into action.

We pray for all the people who, because they did not have a document, had their lives taken from them. This was the situation for many Guatemalan Indigenous families during the war. This was one of the manifestations of the government's ethnocide project. We pray as we see it happen in many other parts of the world as well.

Hear our prayers and lead us into action.

Oramos por todas las personas que por no tener un documento les arrebataron su vida. Lo cual fue la situación de las familias indígenas de Guatemala durante la guerra—el proyecto etnocidio del gobierno. Oramos porque lo vemos pasar en muchas otras partes del mundo también.

Escucha nuestras plegarias y movilizanos a actuar.

Oramos por todas las víctimas de violencia doméstica y de género.

Escucha nuestras plegarias y movilizanos a actuar.

We pray for all victims of domestic and gender violence.

Hear our prayers and lead us into action.

We pray for all lost to inhumane working conditions. We especially name today, the New York Taxi Workers Alliance, as their drivers are on day twelve of their hunger strike.

Hear our prayers and lead us into action.

Oramos por todos los que han muerto trabajando en condiciones inhumanas. Especialmente hoy nombramos a la Alianza de Taxistas de Nueva York, ya que sus conductores están en el día 12 de su huelga de hambre.

Escucha nuestras plegarias y movilizanos a actuar.

Oramos por los que murieron debido a la falta de atención médica en los hospitales agotados de recursos debido a la codicia humana.

Escucha nuestras plegarias y movilizanos a actuar.

We pray for those lost due to lack of health care or depleted hospitals due to human greed.

Hear our prayers and lead us into action.

We pray for those who died of hunger in a world of abundance.
Hear our prayers and lead us into action.
Oramos por los que murieron de hambre en un mundo de abundancia.
Escucha nuestras plegarias y movilizanos a actuar.

Oramos por aquellos que murieron en el frío debido a la falta de refugio como resultado de la codicia humana cuando hay suficientes lugares para que todos podamos dormir sin frío cada noche.
Escucha nuestras plegarias y movilizanos a actuar.
We pray for those who died in the cold due to lack of shelter, a result of human greed when there are enough places for all of us to sleep warmly each night.
Hear our prayers and lead us into action.

We pray for those we've lost to a lack of access to mental health services.
Hear our prayers and lead us into action.
Oramos por aquellos que hemos perdido por falta de acceso a servicios de salud mental.
Escucha nuestras plegarias y movilizanos a actuar.

Oramos por aquellos enterrados en los Potter's Field—campos donde entierran ya sea a cuerpos no reclamados o a personas que no pueden pagar un entierro. Sabemos que muchas veces esto es el resultado del sistema capitalista lleno de codicia en el que vivimos. Oramos para que sus vidas y su humanidad sean recordadas.
Escucha nuestras plegarias y movilizanos a actuar.
We pray for those buried in Potter's fields as either unclaimed bodies or individuals who could not afford a burial. We know that many times this is a result of the greed-filled capitalist system we live in. May their lives and humanity be remembered.
Hear our prayers and lead us into action.

We pray for the many lives lost in the ocean during the Middle Passage in which people from the continent of Africa were forcibly removed from their lands and transported as part of the transatlantic slave trade.

Hear our prayers and lead us into action.

Oramos por las vidas perdidas en el océano durante el *Middle Passage*. Etapa en que personas del continente de África fueron arrebatados de sus tierras y transportados a la fuerza como parte de la trata triangular de esclavos hacia las Américas.

Escucha nuestras plegarias y movilizanos a actuar.

Oramos por las almas inocentes que fueron tomadas y continúan siendo tomadas como sacrificio para el imperio. Que no haya ni una más.

Escucha nuestras plegarias y movilizanos a actuar.

We pray for the innocent souls who were taken as a sacrifice to empire. May there be no more.

Hear our prayers and lead us into action.

Now, a moment for you to name any other prayers you may have. Ahora, un momento para que nombren cualquier otra oración que tengan.

REFLECT, EMBODY, DISCUSS

1. How does the Freedom Church of the Poor challenge the dominant cultural narratives around death and memory?
2. When we practice these rituals of remembrance in communities affected by violence, poverty, and systemic racism, what happens to dominant narratives?
3. How do you grieve? What rituals do you already have within your own tradition that honor and connect you to those who have passed? How might you incorporate the themes and practices discussed in this story into your own life or community work?

LONGEST NIGHT OF THE YEAR: THE STORY

The winter solstice, December 21, marks the longest night of the year and has traditionally been a time for celebrations of renewal and the return of light. However, for many, especially those organizing among poor and unhoused people in the United States, it signifies something deeper. December 21 has become known as National Homeless Persons' Memorial Day, a day to honor those who have lost their lives to the harsh realities of homelessness and the systemic injustices that perpetuate it. On this night, communities gather for candlelight vigils, community gatherings, and religious services, all aimed at mourning, reflection, and collective action. The Longest Night Memorials give voice to those whom society chooses to forget.

National Homeless Persons' Memorial Day has its roots in the struggles and organizing efforts of poor and homeless families across the United States. The National Union of the Homeless (NUH), formed during the economic downturns of the late 1980s and early 1990s, played a pivotal role in establishing this annual memorial. NUH emerged to combat the rising homelessness among families and former workers, using shelters, encampments, and abandoned buildings as centers of organizing. Their efforts aimed to promote social and economic justice, challenging stereotypes with slogans like "You Only Get What You Are Organized to Take!" and "Homeless Not Helpless!"

One significant organizing drive, known as the NUH's Winter Offensive, highlighted the deadly conditions faced by the homeless during winter, a season marked by capitalist commercialism and superficial charity. Out of the NUH organizing efforts, broader coalitions like the National Coalition for the Homeless and the National Health Care for the Homeless Council, which supported and advocated for the rights and needs of the homeless community, began holding annual events on December 21 to honor and remember individuals who died while experiencing homelessness.

Today, homelessness remains a national emergency in the United States, with estimates suggesting that between eight million and eleven million people are homeless, facing precarious conditions on the streets, in shelters, in encampments, and in temporary accommodations. Despite the severity of this issue, it is often ignored or rendered invisible. In response, the Committee to Reestablish the NUH convened in June 2019 to address the growing reality of homelessness. By 2020, the NUH was revitalized and establishing multiple local groups, including the Lancaster Homeless Union in Pennsylvania.

The Lancaster Homeless Union was born from organizing efforts that began in December 2018. Leaders from the South Central Healthcare Rights Committee of Put People First! PA came together to address the impending closure of the St. Joseph Hospital in Lancaster, marking a significant shift in community organizing by connecting health care and housing crises in a fight for human rights. One year later, the Lancaster Homeless Union held their first Longest Night Memorial.

At this memorial, Matt Rosing shared the story of Gregory Baynes, a homeless man with schizophrenia who was killed by police. Matt's testimony underscored the broader issue of systemic neglect and the criminalization of homeless people. Matt, who had experienced homelessness and mental health issues himself, reflected on how Gregory's fate could have been his own. His testimony opened space for others to share their stories, breaking the shame and isolation that often accompany poverty and homelessness.

This fusion style of organizing, which connects various issues and communities, has been key for the Lancaster Homeless Union. It allowed them to respond effectively when crises emerged, such as the city's 2019 plan to shut off water services before Christmas, which would have led to family evictions. Tammy Rosing, a leader of the

Homeless Union, explained that the connections they were making in their organizing were new for the city and caused significant nervousness among officials. The union's ability to draw attention to these crises facing the poor and unhoused and to pressure the city to abandon its plans demonstrated the power of people coming together across issues to organize.

In 2023, the Lancaster Homeless Union's memorial coincided with an announcement from the Department of Housing and Urban Development (HUD), of rising homelessness and Medicaid cuts in the state. Collaborating with organizations in nearby Columbia, the memorial linked struggles for health care, housing, and LGBTQIA2S+ rights. Building connections across communities in Lancaster County was an important strategy for organizers to push back against neoliberal economic policies of local "progressive" governments and the rise of white Christian nationalism in the region.

During the memorial, Jacob Butterly of Put People First! PA, and Deklan Rupp, the coordinator at the Rivertown Pride Center, highlighted the connection of these issues and lifted up the recent deaths of Thea and River, two transgender youth in the community. Parker Webb of Lititz Chooses Love further explained that the deaths of homeless transgender youth, as well as the deaths of those in all historically marginalized communities, too often go unnoticed. Together, the group lifted up the lives of those they'd lost and committed to choose love over hate and people over profit.

The Longest Night of the Year Memorial is a poignant reminder of the human cost of systemic injustice. It honors those who have died while challenging us to envision and work toward a society that values every life. By coming together in remembrance and action, we affirm our commitment to human rights and our determination to end the cycles of poverty and homelessness. We work to build a world where all can live free from fear and hatred, honoring those lost by continuing to unite and organize for human rights for all.

LONGEST NIGHT OF THE YEAR: THE PRAYER

This prayer was written by Rev. Tim Seitz Brown for the Lancaster Homeless Union's 2023 Longest Night of the Year Memorial and read by Matt Rosing.

Creator, I walked into this Rivertown Pride Center
And I should have taken off my shoes for this is truly holy ground
These stories shared
The wisdom shared
But most of all the beauty of each person and this whole community together
Bind us together
Make us strong
We know that one stick by itself is easily snapped
But if we keep adding these sticks, these people together
We will be so strong that the system will not be able to snap us in two
Be with us in these next days
In the coming year
Multiply the work of each person gathered here today
May we treasure one another
May we see each other as a gift
And I remember that moment when I walked in
Who is included in everybody
We know that when we lift from the bottom, everyone rises
Be with us as we commend these people to your love
Help us to fight like hell for the living!

REFLECT, EMBODY, DISCUSS

1. How did the Lancaster Homeless Union and local organizations connect the struggles for health care, housing, and LGBTQIA2S+ rights? Why is this interconnected approach significant?

2. How does the organizing of the Homeless Union challenge the prevailing stereotypes about poverty and homelessness? How does this connect with your experience and understanding of the systemic issues contributing to homelessness?
3. How does Rev. Tim Seitz Brown's prayer reflect the themes of unity and resilience in the face of systemic injustice? What aspects of the prayer do you find particularly meaningful or inspiring?

CHAPTER TWO

HEALING AND TRANSFORMATION

IN THE FACE of injustice, isolation, pain, and suffering, we have a collective responsibility to care for one another and work together to bring about a different world. Civil rights activist Faya Rose Touré's song echoes through our hearts: "We're gonna lift our people up, they are not heavy. If we don't lift them up, we will fall down." 🌐

This sentiment resonates in our bones as we reflect on what it means to build the Freedom Church of the Poor, a community bound by a commitment to mend the deep wounds of our broken world. These wounds are evident in our individual and communal lives, affecting our physical, mental, moral, political, and social well-being. In a society that prioritizes profit over people and the planet, the Freedom Church tradition emphasizes the creation of spaces for care and healing, guiding us toward the Beloved Community and the struggle for social transformation.

In the Freedom Church of the Poor, our focus is on confronting the intersecting evils of poverty, systemic racism, ecological devastation, militarism, and the rise of Christian nationalism. These forces cause immense suffering in poor and marginalized communities, while fostering division to maintain power for the few. The death-dealing effects of these systemic injustices are clear: food insecurity affecting over half of American children, the desecration of sacred Indigenous lands, the trauma experienced by unhoused individuals during violent sweeps, the preventable deaths caused by the lack of affordable health care, and more. Alongside these unlivable conditions, we witness extremist policies rooted in Christian nationalism, which contradict the basic tenets of justice in the Christian tradition to welcome immigrants, free the captives, and lift the load of poverty.

How do we acknowledge the deep wounds created by these systems of injustice while refusing to succumb to fear or despair? Healing practitioners and faith-rooted organizers Teresa Mateus and Vahisha Hasan offer a compelling answer: "Social justice organizing is actually healing work." The Freedom Church tradition seeks to create a space where truths can be shared and we can remind each other that we are not alone, that poverty is not inevitable, and that white supremacy, patriarchy, and heteronormativity do not have the last word. Our approach to transformational healing is holistic—we work to meet people's immediate needs while also fighting to change unjust systems so that everyone can enjoy the abundance of this world. Our aim is to sustain and support leaders for the long haul.

Central to our mission is the act of making the invisible visible. We refuse to allow our people to be dehumanized or marginalized. Through rituals, prayers, songs, and actions, we celebrate the beauty and dignity inherent in every person, reclaiming narratives that highlight our interconnectedness with one another and the earth. As we embark on this healing journey together, we embrace humility and social solidarity. We recognize that leadership is not bestowed upon us but cultivated through shared experiences, mutual support, and right relationships. In the Freedom Church of the Poor, we honor the sacredness of each person, ensuring that everyone has the right to be seen, heard, and respected. Amid adversity, we draw strength from one another. We surround ourselves with images, songs, prayers, and practices that affirm our communities and our capacity to care for one another and heal our society. The words of the prophet Isaiah inspire us: "If you get rid of unfair practices, quit blaming victims, quit gossiping about other people's sins, If you are generous with the hungry and start giving yourselves to the down-and-out, Your lives will begin to glow in the darkness. . . . You'll be known as those who can fix anything, restore old ruins, rebuild and renovate, make the community livable again" (Isaiah 58:9–12 MSG).

Together, we are a force for change—a beacon of hope in a world that too often seeks to divide us. Yet the path to collective healing and social transformation is fraught with obstacles. In a world riven by deep divisions—where families are separated at borders, communities are pitted against each other, and individuals are isolated by poverty and a culture of individualism—our sense of belonging is fragile and fleeting. In these fractured times, rituals of intentionality and solidarity become a vital lifeline.

The Freedom Church tradition calls for the creation of intentional practices for collective gathering, reflection, and action. We must continually affirm the sanctity of our lives and our shared responsibility to uplift and care for one another. Rituals in this context are conduits for creating a different world, one rooted in compassion, empathy, and mutual support. Today, we must reject the myth of individualism and embrace the truth of our interconnectedness. It is only by dismantling barriers and cultivating spaces of belonging and collective action that we can begin to heal the wounds of our society and build a world where all are valued and celebrated for their inherent worth.

This chapter explores four practices of healing and transformation, each a powerful resource that can help to sustain our communities and lay the foundational stones of social transformation.

Foot Washing: In a society where the poor are often blamed for their own suffering, creating space to share our stories becomes a revolutionary act of resilience and empowerment. But how do we navigate the terrain of collective healing when the very notion of community feels elusive and the systems around us are designed to keep us isolated? This ritual of foot washing, rooted in the tradition of Jesus, who washed his disciples' feet, is an act of radical listening and of honoring sacred connections. Washing someone's feet is a subversive act in a society that deems poor and dispossessed people disposable. As Moses Hernandez McGavin, an organizer with the Nonviolent Medicaid Army (NVMA) in Atlanta, Georgia, puts it, when we wash one another's feet, we become reminders that "God shares our wounds."

Gathering in the Garden: The current political landscape hinders genuine community building. Manufactured division, an overreliance on virtual interactions, and the erosion of trust in institutions and one another are major challenges for the building of social movements. The privatization of public spaces has reduced opportunities for social engagement, while the criminalization of poverty further marginalizes vulnerable communities. Amid these obstacles, regularly showing up for one another is a radical form of resistance and affirmation, particularly in marginalized communities. This ritual of gathering in a garden in Brooklyn—or anywhere—highlights mutual aid as a powerful antidote to feelings of worthlessness among those in impacted communities. In a society where the voices of the poor and dispossessed are often drowned out, the simple act of showing up for one another can be revolutionary.

Indigenous Prayer of Gratitude: The concept of healing extends beyond physical wounds to encompass spiritual, emotional, and societal realms. Through prayer, we align our hearts, minds, and souls in pursuit of collective healing and lasting transformation. Healing is a dynamic interplay between the material and the spiritual—a continuous cycle of engagement, reflection, and action. In this chapter we learn a prayer in Nahuatl and English that helps us give thanks for the gift of life and cultivates a holistic approach to healing that encompasses both individual well-being and collective flourishing. In doing so, we honor the inherent interconnectedness of all existence and strive toward a world characterized by harmony, justice, and wholeness.

Health Care Vigil: Our individual well-being is intricately linked to the well-being of others and our society as a whole. The Freedom Church tradition aligns with the long arc of justice in which leaders across movement history have cried out, "*no more!*" No more will we accept that our children are dying because they lack adequate access to health care. No more will we allow health care workers to work endless hours while they themselves have no access to health care. No more will we allow poverty and economic insecurity to prevail in a land of plenty. Collective action, such as the health care vigil described in this chapter, becomes a vehicle for transformation when we organize to address systemic issues like access to health care, economic inequality, racial injustice, and environmental degradation.

In a society that either pities the poor through individual acts of charity or criminalizes their very existence, the rituals and practices emerging from the Freedom Church tradition ground us in the need for broad social transformation. The words of the Peace Poets remind us that the solidarity forged through these rituals is an antidote to the bootstrap ideologies of our world: "Your liberation is my liberation and my liberation is your liberation." 🌐

FOOT WASHING: THE STORY

In the heart of Atlanta, Georgia, amid the busy streets and towering buildings, sits the Church of the Common Ground—a unique sanctuary founded in the early 2000s with a mission to provide a spiritual home for those who might otherwise be turned away. This Episcopal congregation, led by Rev. Kim Jackson, operates as a church without walls, offering a beacon of hope and refuge for the unhoused and marginalized. The church embodies inclusivity and compassion, welcoming all who seek solace and community.

One of the cornerstones of their ministry is the foot washing ritual—a humble yet profound practice that symbolizes humility, compassion, and connection. Every Tuesday, the Church of the Common Ground operates its foot clinic. Housed in a converted storage van, volunteers gather to provide much-needed foot care to the unhoused population. If you are unhoused, you walk a lot. Even if there is good transportation in your community, day in and day out, you spend many hours of the day walking. You are also likely to only have one or two pairs of shoes, if any. And with all the walking you do, you quickly wear out shoes.

The foot clinic emerged as a practical response to this need, reflecting a principle of the Freedom Church tradition: organizing must be rooted in the conditions of poor and dispossessed communities. It is through survival projects that people's needs are met, relationships are built, and efforts to change the conditions that produce poverty and suffering are organized.

The Church of the Common Ground established a Common Soles foot clinic. It grew out of community practices and became a way to connect and build relationships with unhoused people in Atlanta. Foot clinic is a space where people who are living on the streets can come to relax and refresh themselves. Organizers draw inspiration from the passage in Genesis where Abraham says to some weary travelers, "Let a little water be brought, and wash your feet, and rest yourselves under the tree" (Genesis 18:4).

Yet the foot clinic is not just about tending to physical ailments; it's about creating a space for intimacy, vulnerability, and connection. As individuals come forward to have their feet washed, a sacred bond is formed between the caregiver and the one receiving care. In this intimate setting, stories are shared, burdens are lightened, and prayers are offered for healing and strength.

For Moses Hernandez McGavin, ministry coordinator with the Church of the Common Ground, the foot clinic has been a lifeline—a place where he feels seen, heard, and valued. Every time Moses washes someone's feet, he is reminded of our inherent worth and dignity as human beings.

Washing someone's feet is a countercultural act in a society that often deems poor and dispossessed people as disposable. Moses explains that exchanging names is one of the first things that happens at Common Soles. Naming is a sacred act in this community, where unhoused people are often dismissed, ignored, and made invisible. Across their ministries, the intentional practice of asking and reading people's names reclaims dignity and forges deep relationships. This connection fosters an ethic of care that responds to both physical and spiritual needs.

One of the things Moses loves most about this ritual action is the time that it takes to care for someone's feet. It is not a brief interaction. People get to know one another—their journeys, families, challenges, and joys. The ritual of foot washing becomes a tangible way to care for another person and to understand what it means to walk a mile in someone else's shoes.

As a foot washing session concludes with the last prayers offered, a profound sense of gratitude and connection fills the space. In this sacred environment, where wounds are tended and hearts are opened, the community embodies the transformative power of love. It is a testament to the enduring presence of grace for one another in the midst of tremendous hardship and struggle.

For those facing relentless displacement and criminalization at the hands of the city, stable community spaces where genuine relationships can be formed are essential. People need to know there is a place to return to—a place where people will continue to organize for our right to not only survive but to build the Beloved Community. Moses learned that prayer is an act of radical listening—to God and to others. In this exchange, prayer becomes an affirmation, a way to wrap one another in love and care, and a reminder to continue fighting for a society where the beauty and dignity of all people are lifted up.

"Brothers and sisters, siblings in Christ, I have good news," says the Common Ground call to worship. "God is here, God is right here with us, and this is holy ground."

FOOT WASHING: THE PRAYERS

Moses Hernandez McGavin has kept a prayer journal about the foot clinic, and some entries are included here. This practice helped ground him before volunteering at the foot clinic each week. Every Tuesday morning, Moses would light his prayer candles at his altar, say the Lord's Prayer, the Hail Mary, and St. Francis's Prayer, and he would write an entry in his journal to God. These journal entries may help you imagine creating your own prayer journal or what a practice that symbolizes humility, compassion, and connection might look like in your context.

Dear God,

What a weekend, and what a day yesterday. Foot clinic really warmed my heart and lifted my spirits. I feel really called to that work, but I'm also not sure what that looks like, and I want to gain experience and stability before I fully take this on.

So first I want to lift up the prayers of those at foot clinic that I worked with yesterday.

Kevin and his continued search for a home in Clayton County. Adam, watch over him and protect him every day in the streets and continue to walk with him in search of housing and a place to stay. Robert, that you may continue to walk with him and be by his side for protection and to continue to fill his spirit and protect his soul.

And prayers for all those who joined us at foot clinic, including myself. May we be continually protected and watched over, and may you bless our feet as we walk on them and use them every single day. May you help keep us strong but afford rest whenever you can.

. . . Today I look for patience, strength and courage. Give me patience and gratitude as I continue to work my job and give me courage as I talk about this new job today. Thank you God, for giving the world things like theater and thank you for music, monasteries, Sunday mass, and so much more.

In your holy name,

Amen

Dear God,

It's a new year, and a new foot clinic. My prayer to you is to make sure that I go slowly today. Take my time with each person and know what I can and can't do. Help me start a new conversation where I listen more than anything. And just help each individual who walks through that room to be seen and heard by Common Ground. Be in our spirit and in our heart. In this troubled and sick society, walk with us and help us know that we are loved and cared for.

This is what I ask for in your name, God.

Today we give special thanks for community. I was so fortunate to be surrounded by community this weekend, and today we get to make community at Common Ground, and I get to see friends today and make community with them. Today I ask that you give special blessings to everyone that serves today, watch over our spirits, hearts, families, and continued journeys to safety.

Prayers for Mr. Clark, his family, and his journey toward securing housing, and being able to move forward. Prayers for Noah, his family, his continued sobriety, and please be with him in his search of housing. Prayers for Emily; may she continue to be filled with your spirit and protection, and may she find community wherever she is. Prayers for Ronald, who I met yesterday—watch over him and help him be nourished and loved.

May we be filled with your spirit toward a promise of a better world.

Be with us today in community.

Amen

Dear God,

Good morning! Today I am really tired. I tried to wake up early today, but my body and eyes are tired. Today is foot clinic, and the first thing that I'm praying for is for me to wake up! Foot clinic is hard when I feel tired, so I'm praying that I can come back to life a little bit.

One thing that I ask you to work through with me today is to make people smile and laugh. I want to bring a positive and loving energy, and I want to make people feel seen and heard, and I want to continue to get to know folks. Please continue to bless all my friends at foot clinic: Matthew, Matthew, Matt, Shereetha, Chris, Ginger, Patty, Miss Jenn, Thomas, Miss Bertha, and David.

And special blessings for Brad who I was able to meet last week. May you continue to watch over him, keep him safe, and help him find the security and peace he may be seeking. Continued prayers for Anthony, Malcolm, Mr. Frank, and Ashton. Prayers for all the folks I haven't been able to see in a long time. Please work through me to make today a beautiful one.

Amen

REFLECT, EMBODY, DISCUSS

Prayers of gratitude are an important part of our rituals. Why? Because in work that can feel difficult, tiring, and scary, it's easy to slip into the anxieties, fear, or anger that may arise. But gratitude helps us ground ourselves in how fortunate we are to be in this work, what wonderful things and people we come across, and it reminds us of all the good things in our lives.

For prayers of gratitude, set aside a routine practice to do this prayer. It can be once a week, once every couple of weeks, or every day. Record what you are grateful for (either in a voice memo or by writing things down). Here are a couple of broad prompts to get you started.

1. **What are you grateful for?** *It doesn't have to be something major or deeply profound.*
2. **Who are you grateful for?** *Who made you smile this week? Who did you learn more about? Who is someone that is just on your mind? You can name many people or hold a couple in deep prayer.*
3. **Why are you grateful for what you just wrote down?** *Gratitude prayers should dig deeper than just a simple gratitude list. It's a time*

for reflection. What do things and people bring to your life? What do they mean to you?

4. **What are prayers you may have for those things or people you may be grateful for?** *Write down the prayers that you want to lift to God. It may also help to remind you to check in on those that you love.*

GATHERING IN THE GARDEN: THE STORY

Early in the pandemic, leaders of Domestic Workers United (DWU), a grassroots organization of Caribbean, African, and Latinx domestic workers building power and demanding their rights in New York City, swiftly recognized the multifaceted impact of the crisis. They responded by initiating Know Your Rights Zoom sessions, offering vital information and support on health and employment issues during the global pandemic. While these virtual meetings were valuable, members of the DWU community also longed for physical connection and tangible support.

To address this need, DWU partnered with the Maple Street Community Garden in Brooklyn, forging a path of solidarity and care. Initially, this collaboration aimed to meet the basic need for food. Every week, DWU members and volunteers from the garden distributed twenty-five to thirty bags of healthy, sustainable food to women in the DWU community. But as they came together week after week and word spread, more people learned about this food distribution project or saw folks gathering in the garden and they began distributing sixty, seventy, and even eighty bags each week.

The garden soon evolved into more than just a site for food distribution; it became a ritual meeting place of healing and transformation. DWU members from across the city and neighborhood residents converged at the garden to find community, share stories, laugh, and dance. They came to get medicinal teas and homemade wine that members of the community made and sold. The garden became a place to come together and rebuild collective strength, reminding everyone that caring for each other physically, spiritually, and materially was essential.

Christine, a longtime leader of DWU, shared that in coming to the Maple Street Community Garden, the community gathered was seeking to "come back to the garden"—the garden of Eden—to a way of life where all needs were met. "We came to the garden to celebrate life. This gathering time became a ritual for our community." The ritual of gathering in the garden was about refusing to let the struggles of daily life and the dominance of death leave people in fear and isolation.

Central to this community was Denise, a beloved member who started coming to the garden after losing her job because of the pandemic. Denise began making and selling homemade wine, a practice she brought from her home country. During this time, Denise grew sick, and the community learned she had cancer. As her illness got worse, there were days when she would come to the garden when she was not feeling well, and Christine would tell her, "Denise, you don't need to come; stay home and take care of yourself." But Denise would still come. Even when she could not talk, she would come to the garden to sit and listen. The community provided her with the support she needed, both spiritually and emotionally.

The garden became a source of spiritual healing for Denise. She needed the soul of the community to hold her during this time. She needed, as Christine called it, the "medicine from the yard." The garden held the natural healing practices that came from the community and had been passed down from generation to generation; the sustainable food that was distributed to community members; and most importantly the medicine of the community that gathered to share stories, resources, songs, and laughter.

When Denise passed away, Christine spoke at her funeral about the power of Denise's witness and movement leadership and her willingness to show up for things that matter. The ritual that evolved in the garden reflected this intentional practice of showing up.

The garden became a sacred space for those who gathered and pushed past the temptation to turn inward in the heights of the pandemic. To hold space and to show up is about commitment. And commitment is about being dedicated to the task at hand. One of the core meanings of the word *dedicate* is to "devote," or to "make something holy." The community that gathered in the garden were doing something holy by choosing to show up over and over again for one another.

In the end, the garden was not merely a physical space but a sacred sanctuary where the bonds of community were forged and the human spirit was nourished.

GATHERING IN THE GARDEN: THE PRAYER/POEM

Coming Back to The Garden Post Covid 19/A Song for Denise Williams—04/04/63–08/29/24 by Christine Lewis, Domestic Workers United, Brooklyn, NY.

Fear, Mayhem, Madness
A fallen world, some thought
We made it, women with warm calypso accent echoed loudly
By the Grace of God, we made it!!!
Huddled on garden chairs beneath a huge weeping willow tree which weep ever so often
One woman wipes away a tear from her arm
Women who double as home health aides and nannies navigate
The terrains of going to work and coming to receive a food bag
With sustainable fruits and produce from a fertile garden pregnant
With herbs for what ails. Lemongrass, peppermint leaves, Spanish thyme, hot peppers, bitter

gourds and whatever the woman with rhythm in her limbs could find to heal
A community sits beneath the weeping willow tree at Maple Street Community Garden
Talk of love, loss, lack of wages fought for and won, immigration, green cards, and politics
Politics foreign to them with the understanding that politicians play politricks
Yearning for a community away from the community they left behind on Caribbean Soil
A community who will stand with us throughout the changing scenes of life.
A community void of tricks, scam, and fraud
A community who will go with us
A community who will continue to meet under the weeping willow tree for eight Saturdays in
summer and renew food bags even in fall. So needed
To hold up each other's hand
To encourage another with a word or song
Or, who will go for us if we don't go for ourselves
Even when the days seem dark and dreary
For Denise the days were dark and dreary
She showed up to the very end
Showing us what it means to belong to a community.
Hebrews 12:12–13:
12: Wherefore lift up the hands which hang down and the feeble knees.
13: And make straight paths for your feet, lest that which is lame be turned out the way, but let it
rather be healed.
In other words, we are called to care, encourage and lift up each other and not get weary nor
lose heart in doing so.

REFLECT, EMBODY, DISCUSS

1. What do you think made the Maple Street Community Garden such a powerful symbol of resilience and community during the pandemic?
2. How does the ritual of gathering in the garden help individuals like Denise cope with their challenges, both physically and spiritually?
3. In what ways could the values of communal support and shared resources demonstrated in the garden be applied to other communities facing similar crises? What aspects of the Maple Street Community Garden could be replicated or adapted in your community to foster healing and resilience?

AN INDIGENOUS OFFERING OF GRATITUDE: THE STORY

The northeast San Fernando Valley is home to a rich tapestry of Mexican and Central American heritage. It also faces numerous challenges, including economic disparities and cultural isolation. With a significant portion of the population grappling with the effects of trauma, dispossession, and isolation, the community is hungering for connection and expression.

In 2001, Luis J. Mixcoatl Itztlacuiloh Rodriguez and Trini Tlazohteotl Rodriguez, along with their brother-in-law Enrique Sanchez, founded Tía Chucha's Centro Cultural & Bookstore, which offers a sanctuary for healing and creative growth. It is a comprehensive cultural and literacy center in the San Fernando Valley section of Los Angeles. Tía Chucha's has become a crucial cultural and educational hub in the region. Through its focus on ancestral knowledge, the arts, literacy, and creative engagement, the center embodies a holistic approach to community empowerment.

Luis is a renowned writer, with seventeen published books, and Trini is a respected community healer who facilitates a women's sweat lodge circle and community-based Indigenous teachings. Upon returning to the San Fernando Valley from Chicago, Luis and Trini were struck by the stark absence of cultural spaces reflective of their community's narratives and voices. The dearth of bookstores, art galleries, and cultural centers spoke volumes about the systemic exclusion their people faced. Driven by a desire to fill this void, they embarked on the creation of a place where the community could find reflection, expression, and solidarity, and create change together.

Given that 67 percent of the Valley's population identifies as Latino, many of whom are migrants from Mexico or Central Americans with Indigenous roots, Tía Chucha's mission resonates deeply. Luis and Trini note that many Latinos are "detribalized," disconnected from their Indigenous identities due to colonialism and modern displacement. Tía Chucha's serves as a vital bridge back to those roots, offering a space where individuals can rediscover and reclaim their ancestral wisdom and cultural heritage.

The center offers a wide array of workshops and activities, from writing, painting, and music to *Danza Azteca* and natural healing circles, all aimed at nurturing the whole person and building community. Through storytelling and creative expression, Tía Chucha's fosters communal and individual healing, breaking down the walls of isolation and alienation. It is through these shared experiences and explorations of identity that Tía Chucha's cultivates a sense of belonging and collective resilience.

As Tía Chucha's Centro Cultural & Bookstore continues to thrive, it stands as a testament to the transformative power of culture, community, and connection. In a world where such values are increasingly under threat, the center serves as a model. Through its work, Tía Chucha's not only transforms the northeast San Fernando Valley; it offers an example for communities everywhere to reclaim their cultural richness and collective strength.

AN INDIGENOUS OFFERING OF GRATITUDE: THE PRAYER

This Indigenous prayer was offered by Luis J. Mixcoatl Itztlacuiloh Rodriguez and Trini Tlazohteotl Rodriguez, cofounders of Tía Chucha's Centro Cultural & Bookstore.

"Tlazohkamati Ometeotl, Tlazohkamati Tonatiuh, Tlazohkamati Tonantzin, Tlazohkamati Ehecatl, Tlazohkamati Coyolxauhqui . . ."

"Thanks to the Creator, thanks to Father Sun, thanks to Mother Earth, thanks to Brother Wind, thanks to Sister Moon—and all the energies and elements, our relationships, that aligned so we can all be together, in ceremony, for health and well-being of all."

Reflection by Luis J. Mixcoatl Itztlacuiloh Rodriguez and Trini Tlazohteotl Rodriguez

The above prayer is one I've used in Nahuatl and English to give thanks. The Mexica—what some people call Aztec—are people of song, dance, story, poetry, and ceremony. Gratitude is something to acknowledge not just as feeling but an important daily practice.

As Indigenous people, we start with relationality and reciprocity. We honor and respect the elements, the energies, the ancestors, all beings, present, past, and future. This world and the "other world." We don't do this as worship. We are one with them. We don't separate these elements, energies, and beings as if they were above or beyond. They are around us and in us.

For Indigenous people, all prayer is about healing. For wholeness. For balance in times of deep imbalance. For realignment. People and nature are already whole, but with trauma, abandonment, and betrayal, we feel fragmented, alienated, detached. We feel broken. The idea of prayer is to become integrated again, not a split person, or family, or community—or society. Poverty is trauma. Poverty is wholly avoidable. It does not need to exist. But with capitalist relations, people are forced to pay to reside on earth. This system creates great wealth but with great inequality. This system is not about shared well-being but the profits of a few at the expense of the many.

In the Mexica traditions, we pray at two levels: personally (individually, alone) and together (in community). When we pray collectively, this is ceremony. Ceremony embodies both individual healing, including from personal, familial, and generational traumas, as well as community/societal/earth healing. Indigenous ceremonies and Mexica *danza* (traditional dance) focus on both prayers for the "small hungers" and prayers for the "big hungers." The small hungers are the individual longings and wounds. The big hungers are for the collective strength and development of community, country, and world. This is again about aligning. We need to address all hungers. Healing integrates us on various and higher levels of wholeness.

For a person, what the Mexica call *In Itztli In Yollotl*, "face and heart," the alignment should be about what's inside of you and what's outside; the essence with the appearance; who you really are with how you represent yourself. In community, it's about a vision to bring about the well-being of everyone, and consequently organizing to create the conditions to meet their material and spiritual needs. One, to survive (healthy and clean food, water, air, shelter, and clothing) and two, to thrive (preventative and other health care, mental treatment, education, spiritual engagement, including all the arts and creative paths such as music, dance, theater, painting, and writing).

This means we become architects of abundance, which requires a proper and respectful relationship with nature. Humans are also nature but with elevated consciousness—not better or dominant. Nature can be more beautiful and bountiful with human care and protection. This is also important with human interactions in meaningful and respectful relationships. And in each person, "abundance" is inexhaustible in our imaginative capacities. We are naturally whole and abundant. There is medicine and abundance everywhere; but we've often lost the sight to see them.

Prayer is also not passive. Prayer is gratitude woven in with intent. Direction. It's heart, mind, and soul aligned. But all prayer requires action. We need prayer in motion. Once an intent is set, a collective breath is taken, we muster words and practices to help inspire to aspire. We can then move forward, organized, with steps to realize the imagination and vision of our prayers. First imagination, then implementation.

Prayer is vital but also not the end. The story is not over. The story continues. All "endings" are beginnings. All stories, even with transformation as an aim, keep going. No closure or "beginning, middle, and end" of Hollywood movies or most books. We are intent on elevating within the spiral of life. This is how we become prayer-in-motion to end poverty.

REFLECT, EMBODY, DISCUSS

1. How does this prayer of gratitude help remind you that the well-being of one part of creation is intricately linked to the well-being of all others? How does this interdependent relationship motivate you to work toward justice for all beings, not just for yourself or your community?
2. Practice mindfulness in your daily activities. What do you notice about how you show up in your community? How are other people in your community showing up? How can we, in our daily lives, take up practices that remind us of and ground us in our relationship to one another and to all creation?
3. Take the time to learn about issues related to social and environmental justice, including the interconnectedness of various forms of oppression and exploitation. Engage with your local community and participate in activities that promote social and environmental justice. This could involve volunteering, advocacy, or supporting local initiatives that address systemic injustices.

HEALTH CARE VIGIL: THE STORY

In October 2020, members of The Open Table KC, the Kansas Poor People's Campaign, and a myriad of allied voices gathered in Pittsburg, Kansas, for a candlelight vigil to lift up the people who had died from the pandemics of COVID-19 and poverty. This day of action served not only as a testament to the lives lost but also as a resounding call to confront the systemic injustices that paved the way for such devastating outcomes. Indeed, crises such as the COVID-19 pandemic do not materialize in isolation; rather, they reveal the deep disparities that underscore the social and economic fabric of our nation. Prior to the pandemic's emergence, the United States was hard at work masking the profound inequities in wealth, income, and access to resources. The devastation wrought by the pandemic exacerbated these preexisting conditions and exposed the urgent need for systemic change.

The vigil in Kansas was an attempt to hold up members of this community in a time of tremendous grief and despair; it also acknowledged that the deadly consequences were not the accidental result of an unforeseen global pandemic, but the compounded results of poverty, economic insecurity, and systemic racism. More people in the United States died from COVID-19 than in any other country. The pandemic's ripple effects extended beyond mere mortality, with an estimated 1.2 million individuals in the United States newly living with disabilities, a stark testament to the multifaceted impact of systemic neglect and inequity.

Policy experts connected to the Poor People's Campaign: A National Call for Moral Revival highlight that these atrocities are linked to inaccessible and inadequate health care resources during the pandemic. For the leaders gathered in Pittsburg, this candlelight vigil was more than a moment of remembrance; it was a clarion call for action. Kansas leaders felt compelled to raise people's consciousness that Kansas health care policies, including the state's refusal to expand Medicaid, directly contributed to needless death and suffering. The leaders who gathered acknowledged that the only path toward healing, the only possibility for hope, was to organize, mobilize, and advocate for transformative change.

As the flickering flames of the vigil illuminated the contradictions of abandonment in a nation of plenty, the group confronted adversity with resilience, despair with action, and injustice with unwavering solidarity. The healing needed in this community—the physical, spiritual, and social healing—could only be achieved by taking up a shared pursuit of justice and equality for all.

HEALTH CARE VIGIL: THE LITANY

This litany was written by the Rev. Dr. Letiah Fraser and Claire Chadwick. As with other liturgies and rituals included in this book, specific information and data points can be adapted to your community.

All: We will continue to organize and fight.

Reader 1: We light this candle in memory of the nearly seven hundred people who die every day in the United States due to lack of access to health care.

All: We will continue to organize and fight.

Reader 2: We light this second candle in recognition of the closure of Central Kansas Medical Center in Great Bend due to the failure to pass Medicaid expansion. We mourn the loss to the community, including lack of access to health care for their community, ease of access, and loss of jobs.

All: We will continue to organize and fight.

Reader 3: We light this third candle in recognition of the closure of Mercy Hospital in Fort Scott due to failure to pass Medicaid expansion. We mourn the loss to the community, including lack of access to health care for their community, ease of access, and the loss of jobs.

All: We will continue to organize and fight.

Reader 4: We light this fourth candle in recognition of the closure of Mercy Hospital Independence due to the failure to pass Medicaid expansion. We mourn the loss to the community, including lack of access to health care for their community, ease of access, and the loss of jobs.

All: We will continue to organize and fight.

Reader 5: We light this fifth candle in recognition of the closure of Oswego Community Hospital due to the failure to pass Medicaid expansion. We mourn the loss to the community, including lack of access to health care for their community, ease of access, and the loss of jobs.

All: We will continue to organize and fight.

Reader 6: We light the sixth candle to acknowledge 60,894 people who have been diagnosed with COVID-19 in the state of Kansas.

All: We will continue to organize and fight.

Reader 7: The seventh candle we light in memory of 678 people who have died from COVID-19 in Kansas so far.

All: We will continue to organize and fight.

Reader 8: We light this eighth candle to acknowledge 1,098 people in Crawford County, Kansas, who have been diagnosed with COVID-19 so far.

All: We will continue to organize and fight.

Reader 9: We light this ninth candle in memory of the eight people who have died from COVID-19 in Clarksburg County, Kansas, so far.

All: We will continue to organize and fight.

Reader 10: We light this tenth candle to acknowledge the 39,965 children between the ages of zero and eighteen who are uninsured in Kansas due to the lack of Medicaid expansion.

All: We will continue to organize and fight.

Reader 11: We light this candle, for the 68,236 adults between the ages of nineteen and sixty-four who are uninsured in Kansas due to the lack of Medicaid expansion.

All: We will continue to organize and fight.

Reader 12: We light this twelfth candle to acknowledge the 694 seniors who are sixty-five or older and are uninsured in Kansas due to a lack of Medicaid expansion.

All: We will continue to organize and fight.

Reader 13: We light the thirteenth candle as we acknowledge the essential workers in Kansas who often become expendable because they are uninsured or underinsured.

All: We will continue to organize and fight.

Reader 14: We light this fourteenth candle to acknowledge those who work in health care, home health care, and our personal care attendants who do not have access to health care.

All: We will continue to organize and fight.

Reader 15: We light the fifteenth candle for over 4,000 attendants who don't have access to health care.

All: We will continue to organize and fight.

Reader 16: We light this sixteenth candle and hope that Medicaid expansion will be passed on campus during the upcoming legislative session.

All: We will continue to organize and fight.

Reader 17: We light the seventeenth candle and hope that everyone who lives in Kansas will be able to access and afford to take care of their health care needs.

All: We will continue to organize and fight.

Reader 18: We light this candle in hope that universal health care will be recognized as a human right in the United States.

All: We will continue to organize and fight.

REFLECT, EMBODY, DISCUSS

1. What emotions does this particular vigil evoke for you? How do you perceive the significance of such collective gatherings in times of crisis?
2. Can you think of examples from your own life or community where collective action has served as a catalyst for positive change and healing?
3. Reflecting on the need for healing through collective action, what steps can you take in your community to address systemic issues such as health care access, economic inequality, racial injustice, and environmental degradation?

CHAPTER THREE

MOURNING

The Freedom Church of the Poor tradition teaches us to gather to wail in sorrow and indignation for the lives lost to poverty, violence, and systemic oppression even as we demand accountability and change. Like Rachel mourning for her children in the book of Jeremiah, we weep for those lost to poverty, the lack of health care, the pandemic, war, gun violence, police brutality, and more. We wail in the face of a system that normalizes the death of two hundred and fifty thousand people every year due to poverty, the fourth leading cause of death in the United States. We mourn that thousands of people are dying unnecessarily because our country fails to provide affordable housing, living-wage jobs, Medicaid expansion, paid sick leave, and other basic human rights that could help guarantee a society where everybody has the right to live and thrive.

Poor and dispossessed people must create spaces to mourn in a society that says that some lives matter less than others. When, in the middle of a global pandemic, the nation deems workers "essential" but fails to give them the essentials they need to survive, we must have the space to weep. In a country that criminalizes homeless people for trying to survive and buries poor and low-income people in mass, unmarked graves (while politicians worry more about the cost of burials than about why people are dying in the first place), we must wail.

Our mourning is a protest, a call to action, and a plea for justice. Our tears are both an expression of grief and a rallying cry—a call to organize against the forces that conspire to rob us of our dignity and our humanity. In our collective mourning, we reject the harsh realities of a society that has normalized the death of its most vulnerable members. We mourn not only for the lives lost but for the spiritual death of a nation that has forsaken its most sacred duty: to protect and uplift every member of its many communities. When we mourn the callous policies of our government, we hear the words of the prophet Isaiah: "Woe to those who make unjust laws, to those who issue oppressive decrees, to deprive the poor of their rights and withhold justice from the oppressed of my people, making widows their prey and robbing the fatherless" (Isaiah 10:1–2 NIV).

Through our acts of collective and public mourning, we find the strength and purpose to say, "No more!" As we remember the fallen, we also demand action. We demand an end to the policies and practices that perpetuate poverty and exploitation. We demand universal health care, decent housing, and equitable opportunities for all. We demand an end to the cycle of violence and neglect that has claimed so many lives. And we disrupt the silence that enables injustice to thrive.

Mourning in the Freedom Church tradition allows us to do several things: (1) Resist systems that dehumanize the poor; (2) Create divine acts of resistance; (3) Celebrate the leadership of those who have fought and died for change; and (4) Commit to changing the systems that perpetuate death and suffering.

In our collective and public mourning—which is grounded in daily struggles of poor and dispossessed people to survive—an audacious hope is ignited. This hope, which is fostered in struggle, is not naive. It emerges from a powerful faith in one another and in the God who hears the cries of the poor for peace, justice, and freedom. By reaching deep into our collective grief and outrage, we can usher in a new era of compassion and justice.

In this chapter, we highlight four rituals and liturgies of mourning. As we lift up those who have died unjustly, we remember, and we refuse to be silent anymore.

The Potter's Field Liturgy: While the ranks of the unhoused continue to grow and death tolls due to poverty are rising in one of the richest countries in the world, poor and homeless people are blamed and shamed for their poverty. Over ten million people live without housing or on the brink of homelessness, while at the same time there are over eighteen million vacant homes across the country. While mortgage debts, increasing rents, and low wages put us all at risk of losing our housing, legislation is being passed and Supreme Court cases are being decided that make homelessness a crime. When people die on the streets, they are often laid to rest anonymously in common plots, in wooden boxes labeled "John" or "Jane Doe." Families are rarely notified, and if they are, they are seldom given access to the gravesite. In spite of this abandonment by the government, poor and dispossessed people have always come together to care for and memorialize one another. Early Christian burial associations stood as symbols of resistance against the dehumanizing practices of the Roman Empire, offering sacred space for collective grief and remembrance. In the Freedom Church tradition, public mourning rituals such as the Potter's Field liturgy become a powerful catalyst for social change. Burial rites for the poor and dispossessed are a form of resistance that decry dehumanizing systems and demand accountability from those in power.

Black Lives Matter Protest: In a world where marginalized communities are disproportionately affected by death-dealing systems of empire, mourning is a radical refusal to allow anyone to be forgotten. In the Freedom Church tradition, there is a collective demand for recognition that everybody has the right to live, which challenges the notion of disposability perpetuated by oppressive structures. Through communal rituals of mourning such as the Black Lives Matter liturgy in this chapter, we honor the lives lost to injustice and reaffirm our commitment to dismantling systems that perpetuate harm. When we come together to mourn, march, grieve, and take action, we transform mere rituals into divine acts of resistance. Collective and public mourning emerges as a potent tool for solidarity, remembrance, and resistance in a world scarred by loss and injustice.

A Eulogy and Bell Ceremony: Our faith in a just God and our belief in the transformative power of those with little or nothing to lose inspire us to take a stand and continue the fight for justice. By honoring the memories of fallen leaders, as we do in the eulogy for Veronica Dorsey and the bell ceremony included in this chapter, we remember the fundamental principles of effective movement leadership: commitment, connection, competence, and clarity. Within the Freedom Church of the Poor tradition, our celebration of bottom-up leadership uplifts poor and dispossessed people who have courageously spoken out against injustice. By celebrating the lives and leadership of those who have chosen to fight with and as those most impacted by injustice in society, we find courage to pick up and carry their baton of justice.

Mourner's Kaddish and Prayer: In this chapter, we read a liturgy created by a national movement of poor and dispossessed people fighting for health care as a human right. These leaders intimately understand the pain of our nation's health care crisis: Many of their friends, family members, and comrades have died because they couldn't afford health care in a system that prioritizes profit over people. By embracing our grief and remembering the powerful lives of these unsung saints, we gain the strength and resolve to fight for a better future. "The more I grieve and mourn, the more I heal and the more energy I have to turn to life," shares Julia Willis, a leader in the Nonviolent Medicaid Army. "Those in power don't want us to have time to mourn or be joyful. They want us to numb out. They don't want us to feel the heaviness of our losses and all the weight of the system upon us, because we will surely do something about it."

Our mourning, our wailing, our tears—these are not signs of weakness but of resilience, of our unwavering dedication to the pursuit of justice. Mourning, in a death-dealing society, is a means of advancing our prophetic stand for justice. As we delve into the transformative power of collective mourning, we will see how it fortifies our spirit, fuels our activism, and unites us in our pursuit of equity and justice.

THE POTTER'S FIELD LITURGY: THE STORY

Hart Island, a small island accessible only by boat, stands off the shore of The Bronx as a somber testament to the forgotten souls of New York City. More than one million individuals, primarily the unknown poor, have found their final resting place in what some call "New York's City of the Forgotten Dead."

For decades, individuals buried here were interred without ceremony, their identities lost to bureaucratic inefficiencies and societal indifference. But through the efforts of Picture the Homeless (PTH), an organization of poor and homeless people organizing for housing and dignity in New York City, and the tireless and persistent organizing and advocacy of concerned clergy and other moral leaders, a transformative movement is honoring the dignity of poor and homeless people who have been laid to rest on Hart Island. (To learn more about Picture the Homeless and the Potter's Field campaign, visit the Picture the Homeless Oral History Project. This project was conducted by Lynn Lewis, former executive director of PTH. It is archived in digital format with the Housing Justice Oral History Project at the New School for Social Research and in digital and analog format with the Tamiment Library and Robert F. Wagner Labor Archives at New York University.)

In August 2004, PTH confronted the tragic reality that one of their own cofounders, Lewis Haggins, had been buried on Hart Island as a John Doe. Haggins had died on the subway after falling ill, and he was laid to rest without his identity being established. His family and community were thus unable to pay their respects.

When PTH leaders shared the news that Haggins had died, Charlie Heck, a member who was street homeless for twenty-seven years when he met PTH, rallied others to ensure that Lewis Haggins be given a "proper Christian burial." While most did not know what had happened to Haggins's remains, Charlie taught other members of PTH about the existence of Potter's Field, or what he called "the prison of the dead," where unknown and unclaimed New Yorkers were buried in mass graves dug by inmates of Rikers Island, New York City's largest jail. Heck, a person of deep faith, had worked to prevent homeless people from being buried at Potter's Field in the past.

Picture the Homeless came together to launch a Potter's Field campaign to ensure that their homeless and poor siblings could have a dignified and spiritual send-off. "In terms of the homeless community, we've got to remember that it is a community," William Burnett, a long-time leader in the organization, explained. "People know each other.... When somebody you have a relationship with, any kind of relationship with, passes away, you're going to feel a loss."

Homeless people "have relationships just like people who are not homeless," Burnett said. "Homeless people are pushed out of society while they're living, and then when they're dead, they're put on an island that nobody can see, and so they're pushed out of society when they're dead too."

Affirming human dignity is at the heart of organizing homeless folks. The Potter's Field campaign was the only campaign at PTH that did not use protest as a tactic. Instead, they built power based on values shared by homeless leaders and faith leaders, and most New Yorkers actually shared their beliefs. Through this campaign, they exposed the way that the city of New York disrespected both the poor who passed away and the poor who sought to mourn their loss. Homeless leaders and faith leaders deeply connected with the family of Lewis Haggins. These relationships enriched the whole community and created opportunities to build political power to win policy change.

During the Potter's Field campaign, leaders of Picture the Homeless came together with seminarians at Union Theological Seminary who had started the Poverty Initiative (now the Kairos Center for Religions, Rights, and Social Justice) to win the right for family and community leaders to visit Hart Island. They also hosted gatherings of community leaders, faith leaders, and seminarians at Union to build relationships and support for the homeless community and for this campaign (all documented in the MDiv thesis of Rev. Amy Gopp).

Building these relationships between PTH leaders, seminary students and professors, and faith leaders was a transformative experience for the whole community. Sharing the stories of this struggle and witnessing how homeless leaders refused to let society disrespect and disregard members of their community, unearthed deep moral and biblical challenges to the dehumanizing reality that homeless people experience in life and in death. One Bible professor noted, "I now understand Communion. You know, I've studied for years that the early Christian groups, the churches, were actually burial associations. They were basically groups of poor people who vowed to take care of each other when they died, because they were living in an empire that was both killing poor people and degrading their deaths. When Jesus says, 'Do this in remembrance of me,' that's actually about a tradition of poor people memorializing each other."

During the Potter's Field campaign, leaders came to realize that for most of its history, no memorial services were allowed for those buried on Hart Island. In 2004, when Picture the Homeless and the Poverty Initiative held Lewis Haggins's memorial service at Union Theological Seminary, they expanded the service to honor and remember all those buried in Potter's Field. "These are people who in life were disrespected, abused, pushed aside," PTH leader Rogers reflects. "We're pushing for them to be cared for, respected, in death."

The memorial service became a space for collective mourning, one that reminded us that all life is sacred and that we are called to lift each other up in life and in death. The call to worship (included in this chapter) compares the situation of homeless people today to that of the poor in the Bible. In a midrash of Matthew 27, PTH leaders connected the temple elites who conspired to execute Jesus to the homeless shelters, HMOs, and other institutions which are complicit in the poverty and death of the poor today. They connected Pontius Pilate, the governor who oversaw the crucifixion of Jesus, to the New York Police Department, the Metropolitan Transit Authority, and the Department of Corrections who are responsible for depositing the bodies of the poor and indigent in Potter's Field. They linked Jesus's innocence with the innocence of poor people dying from poverty today. They critiqued the banks, real estate companies, multinational corporations, and even charitable organizations for making their profits on the backs of the poor and dispossessed.

Congregants were invited to write prayers, hopes, or blessings on papers to place on a sheet that hung in the chapel. Responding to the question posed in the opening song, "Are You There When They Bury All the Poor?" (adapted by Rogers from "Were You There"), this sheet of paper was labeled with the words *We Are There.* ⊕

During the service, Dawn Quinones reminded those gathered that "just because we're poor doesn't mean that we should be forgotten." The memorial service deepened a commitment for those gathered to end all dehumanizing systems in this society.

By fostering deep connections between faith leaders and families affected by homelessness, the Potter's Field campaign built solidarity and political power. The campaign also yielded tangible victories. Leaders secured the right for family and community members to visit Hart Island, reclaiming the space as a site for collective mourning and remembrance. The campaign culminated in the establishment of bimonthly memorial services, which now provide an ongoing opportunity to honor the lives lost and uphold the inherent worth and dignity of every individual, both in life and in death.

THE POTTER'S FIELD LITURGY: THE RITUALS

Note: Amy Gopp, a seminarian at the time, and leaders of Picture the Homeless—including William Burnett, Dawn Quinones, Bruce Little, Torrey Sommerville, Rogers, Mike Slater, and Jean Rice—created and led this call to worship as a part of a memorial service for Lewis Haggins and all those buried in Potter's Field. The service was held on March 23, 2005, in James Chapel at Union Theological Seminary.

Call to Worship from Matthew 27:1–10

Leader: "When morning came, all the chief priests and the elders of the people conferred together against Jesus in order to bring about his death."

Voice 1: Who decided that we should die?

Voice 2: Was it the shelter?

Voice 3: Was it the HMO?*

Voice 4: Was it the government?

* Health Maintenance Organization.

Leader: "They bound him, led him away and handed him over to Pilate the governor."

Voice 5: We were found slumped in a subway car,

Voice 6: We were taken by MTA,**

Voice 7: We were handed over to NYPD,***

Voice 1: Who passed us on to the medical examiner,

Voice 2: Who passed us on to the Dept. of Corrections,

Voice 3: Who handed us over to Hart Island

Voice 4: Where we were buried as anonymous units in potter's field.

Leader: "When Judas, his betrayer, saw that Jesus was condemned, he repented and brought back the thirty pieces of silver to the chief priests and the elders."

Voice 5: We're handed over for a whole lot more than thirty pieces of silver;

Voice 6: Thirty-eight thousand of us were handed over to the Dept. of Homeless Services for $700 million last year.

Voice 7: The Volunteers of America, Salvation Army, Help USA, Samaritan Village, and the Doe Fund receive these "pieces of silver"—the $700 million—from the Dept. of Homeless Services.

Leader: "He said, 'I have sinned by betraying innocent blood.' But they said, 'What is that to us? See to it yourself.' "

Voice 1: They handed us over—none of us were guilty, just poor.

Voice 2: But what do they care why we became homeless?

Leader: "Throwing down the pieces of silver in the temple, he departed; and he went and hanged himself."

** Metropolitan Transportation Authority in the New York City metropolitan area.

*** New York Police Department.

Voice 3: But we have seen no remorse in the Judases of our day;

Voice 4: They fling coins into their coffers and into our coffins and carry on.

Leader: "But the chief priests, taking the pieces of silver said, 'It is not lawful to put them into the treasury, since they are blood money.' "

Voice 5: But our temples,

Voice 6: Citibank,

Voice 7: Real Estate,

Voice 1: Wall Street,

Voice 2: Multinational Corporations,

Voice 3: Won't refuse our blood money.

Leader: "After conferring together, they used them to buy the potter's field as a place to bury foreigners."

Voice 4: In 1868 New York City spent $75,000 to purchase Hart Island.

Voice 5: This would become the final resting place for the nameless, indigent, and homeless poor.

Leader: "For this reason that field has been called the Field of Blood to this day."

Voice 6: That is why it is called the Field of Blood to this day.

Leader: "Then was fulfilled what had been spoken through the prophet Jeremiah, 'And they took the thirty pieces of silver, the price of the one on whom a price had been set, on whom some of the people of Israel had set a price, and they gave them for the potter's field, as the Lord commanded me.' "

Voice 7: What's the price paid for the dignity of the dead?

Together: What's the price paid for the dignity of the living poor?

Prayer of Response and Thanksgiving

This prayer, written by William Burnett, followed a time in the memorial service in which those gathered were invited to light a candle and write a name of someone they know or suspect is buried at Potter's Field, or a loved one who died, regardless of where they are buried.

Merciful Father, today we celebrate the lives of our forgotten sisters and brothers in exile who have gone before us to our eternal home. You have not forgotten them. We entrust them to your eternal embrace. But you, Father, are God of the dead—and God of the living. We lay bold claim, today, to your promise of faithful care for the daughters and sons of your Kingdom. You are God who hears the cry of the poor. So we place our hope in you.

You call us, today, to be instruments of your kingdom. Your Son said, "I came to bring fire to the earth, and how I wish it were already kindled!" (Luke 12:49). Make of us worthy kindling for your fire of love and of justice.

We give you thanks, eternal Father, through your Son Jesus Christ who, from Calvary's hill, lifts us up, in unity with the Holy Spirit who comforts us and guides our lives.

Amen.

REFLECT, EMBODY, DISCUSS

1. How familiar were you with the concept of potter's fields, like Hart Island, before reading this story? Did anything surprise you about the treatment of the deceased individuals in these locations? Do you know what happens to the bodies of the unclaimed dead, including homeless, unidentified, and unknown people, where you live?

2. The Potter's Field Memorial Service and campaign highlight the importance of recognizing the humanity and dignity of homeless individuals. How do you think perceptions of homelessness contribute to the neglect of those laid to rest in potter's fields?
3. Reflect on the establishment of bimonthly memorial services on Hart Island. How do you think these rituals of remembrance contribute to collective healing and advocacy for poor and homeless communities?

BLACK LIVES MATTER PROTEST: THE STORY

The music and mission of alternative hip-hop band Flobots has always been to create community and ignite the activist spirit in their listeners. Flobots band members were not afraid to take a stand for justice, joining other political musicians like Zach de la Rocha and Tom Morello from Rage Against the Machine, to march alongside leaders from Iraq Veterans Against the War as they protested outside the 2008 Democratic National Convention, demanding that Barack Obama commit to ending the war. Their 2012 album, *Circle in the Square*, was infused with themes of resistance and solidarity that emerged on the streets during the Arab Spring and Occupy Wall Street.

While Flobots had always taken a political position, during the emergence of the Black Lives Matter movement, their mentor, prominent civil rights leader Dr. Vincent Harding, challenged them to take a more forward role. When George Zimmerman was acquitted in the shooting death of Trayvon Martin, and when Michael Brown in Missouri and Eric Garner in New York were killed by police, Dr. Harding would ask band members Jamie Laurie and Stephen Brackett, "Where are the songs for today's movements?"

When he asked this question, he did not want to know what songs they were working on for their next album. He was asking, *What are you doing in the movement? How are you using your craft to contribute to the movement? And how can you get people to come together for a cause through song?*

In May 2014, Dr. Harding passed away. Jamie and Stephen now knew that they had to create music in and for the movement. Guided by Dr. Harding's spirit and their own sense of purpose, Flobots embarked on a journey to harness the power of music as a unifying force within the movement. They began gathering organizers, artists, and community members to brainstorm songs for specific upcoming actions. These spaces invited everybody to be a songwriter.

As they gathered, they asked: What songs can we sing together? What songs can we build on, and what are the words we already have? How do we change them to match what's happening in the streets? What are the actions coming up? What message is needed? While this practice of collectively building their voice was new, Flobots knew that the conditions in the street and generations of freedom fighters who had lifted freedom songs were behind them.

A defining moment in their activism came in August 2015, on the anniversary of the murder of Michael "Mike" Brown. In a Black Lives Matter march through the streets of Denver, Colorado, the Flobots brought together a movement music formation called the No Enemies Choir, in which community members commemorated lives lost to police violence and racial injustice.

The march was planned to begin at Sonny Lawson Park in a historically Black neighborhood and go to the Denver County Courthouse, where demonstrators placed flowers and mementos on the courthouse steps and listed the names of people killed by law enforcement. This march became a space for the community to publicly mourn the death of Mike Brown on the one-year anniversary. They also mourned local victims like Paul Castaway, who was shot in a trailer park in July 2015; Jessica Hernandez, an unarmed seventeen-year-old shot in a car in an alley; Ryan Ronquillo, a twenty-one-year-old shot outside his friend's funeral; and many more. Victims from other parts of the country were also named, including Eric Garner, Oscar Grant, Freddie Grey, and Sandra Bland. Throughout the city of Denver, names that had been forgotten were being newly lifted up through Black Lives Matter actions. These ritual acts of mourning both remembered the unjust pattern of police violence and affirmed the sacred lives lost at the hands of such violence.

This ritual act was anchored by a song that the No Enemies Choir helped to lead during the march: "We Remember You." The song was just that: the simple refrain "We remember you," held together with layered harmonies and interspersed with the reading of the names of those killed by a system of police violence and racial injustice.

Later, Jamie reflected how this one simple song encapsulated a full range of emotion. "The somberness was fully embodied, and then I remember as we walked back, continuing to sing the song, as people were lifting up names," he said. "By the time we returned to the courthouse, somehow a transformation had taken place. We had moved from this place of deep grief to a shared sense of empowerment—to collective joy at the power of people assembled that day." With each repetition of the chorus and the reading of names, they honored the memory of the fallen and reaffirmed their commitment to the struggle for justice.

In marching, grieving, taking action, and saying their names together, the group refused to allow anybody to be erased. Stephen explains that the song becomes a divine act of resistance: "The words are incredibly simple, but the sentiment is empire toppling. If we keep these people with us, then their losses are not truly losses. Their stories are now mandates for us to change the situation that took them from us."

This simple refrain, "We Remember You," has been used to evoke the deep connections that exist between those killed by state violence, militarism, and the perpetuation of a war economy. Taken up in the calls for permanent ceasefire and liberation in Palestine (2023–2024), it has become a call for solidarity between poor and oppressed people in the United States and the poor and oppressed harmed by imperialism around the world.

Ritual acts like these become a way to summon our elders back with us, to summon the young ones who were taken too soon. Participants in rituals of resistance reclaim the narrative of their communities and assert their right to exist free from violence and oppression. Through the transformative power of music and collective action, we find solace and strength. In this moment, "We Remember You" becomes more than just a song; it becomes a declaration of resistance, a summons to the ancestors, and a pledge to carry forward the work of building a more just and equitable world.

BLACK LIVES MATTER PROTEST: THE SONG

This song was created by the No Enemies Choir (a local movement music group convened by Flobots) and shared in community on the one-year anniversary of Mike Brown's death in Denver, Colorado. 🌐

We remember you
We remember you
We remember you . . .

[*Call out the names of those who have been killed by the systems of police violence and racial injustice.*]

Mike Brown
Paul Castaway
Jessica Hernandez
Ryan Ronquillo
Tamir Rice

We remember you
We remember you
We remember you . . .

Eric Garner
Oscar Grant
Freddie Grey
Sandra Bland

[*Call out the names of the people who we are building a better world for.*]

Damien Jackson
Aaron Johnson
Trisha Coleman
Anton Williams

"We Remember You": The Rap

This rap was written by Jamie Laurie as a tribute to Dr. Vincent Harding.

We remember you . . .

I was on a date when I learned you had passed
Through an email when I checked my phone in the bathroom
Short of breath when I was stepping out
I apologized and went to Stephen's house
Man, we knew it had to happen someday
But on May 19 somebody snatched the sun away
Reflecting on which path we wanted to take
Took a step back and saw that you'd already shown the way
Cause even after death we knew what you'd say
We didn't have to guess or resuscitate
We could feel your presence from beyond
Cause your message to the young activists never fluctuates
Every time you told us you believed in us
You breathed another breath into each of us
Reaching up with gratitude since you died
Cause we never could imagine you remained so alive

We remember you . . .

REFLECT, EMBODY, DISCUSS

1. Consider the power of ritual acts in resistance movements. How do these rituals help communities process grief and trauma while also asserting their demands for justice?
2. Reflect on the significance of commemorating lives lost to systemic violence and injustice. How does remembering and honoring these individuals contribute to the larger struggle for social justice?

3. Reflect on a time when music or art played a significant role in a social or political movement. How did it shape the movement's message or effectiveness?

A EULOGY AND BELL CEREMONY: THE STORY

Veronica Dorsey, a mother, daughter, friend, and low-wage worker, found herself at the heart of a struggle for human dignity and justice at Camden Yards in Baltimore. Her story resonates as a testament to the resilience and power that can be built when poor and low-wage workers come together to fight against systemic injustices.

In the early 2000s, Veronica worked as a cleaner at Camden Yards, earning just $4.50 an hour. "I was working down at Camden Yards making less than a hot dog," she says, in vivid summary of her situation. "I was baffled. I was working really hard cleaning up peanut shells and dirty toilet seats, and my salary was less than a hot dog. I couldn't afford to eat." If she did buy something to eat, Veronica explains, she would be forced to eat in a bathroom she had cleaned or a stadium closet.

Tired of these inhumane conditions and the lack of dignity shown to her on the job, Veronica joined the United Workers (UW), a multiracial organization of low-wage workers dedicated to ending poverty and advocating for human rights. She became part of a movement fighting for living wages and union rights for day laborers at Camden Yards. Veronica's journey with the UW didn't just focus on her own struggles but expanded to empowering others. She became a leadership organizer, nurturing the voices and leadership of fellow low-wage workers in Baltimore.

Veronica's commitment to justice extended beyond the workplace. As a lover of children, she embraced the principle from the welfare rights tradition: "children aren't in the way; they *are* the way," that the Freedom Church of the Poor community still embodies today. At any movement convening, you could find Veronica gathering the children to play a game, to lead a song, and to simply bring love and joy into the struggle. Veronica's message was clear: the only thing they had was each other, and they refused to let their dignity be stripped away any further.

Veronica became a fierce leader who believed in the sacredness of all life. At a 2009 press conference at Baltimore's Inner Harbor, when a local television reporter asked if now was the "right time" for workers to make any demands of employers, given the economic crisis and high levels of unemployment, Veronica quickly responded, "Yes, we feel it is [the right time] because we believe that all life is sacred, and we believe that all humans have the right to be respected and to have human dignity."

This was the spirit Veronica brought to the movement. At organizing meetings in Baltimore and gatherings of poor people's organizations across the country, Veronica was always ready to lift her voice for justice. She would regularly break into a verse of "This Little Light of Mine." Veronica's song was her prayer—a prayer that calls all of us to celebrate the sacred light that shines within each one of us. Too often our light is hidden and diminished by a society that deems poor and low-wealth people to be disposable. But Veronica's passionate, committed, and transformational leadership was an example of the leadership that must be cultivated among poor and dispossessed people, as a force for change in our society.

Veronica died suddenly in 2013. Her death was a profound loss not only to her family and friends but also to the United Workers and the broader movement to end poverty. She was more than just a leader; she was a Poverty Scholar, and the first to graduate from the United Workers three-year intensive leadership development program. She understood that true leadership lies in developing other leaders and building a movement to end poverty and its interlocking injustices.

Leaders like Veronica Dorsey ground us in the liberation tradition and remind us that the lives and leadership of the poor must be celebrated. In mourning the lives of leaders like Veronica, we lift them up among the communion of saints who have paved the way for the Freedom Church of the Poor tradition.

This is why, when the UW launched their Right to Health campaign in 2024, they did so on Memorial Day. As they gathered to affirm that everybody's got a right to health, that everybody's got a right to live, and that everybody's got a right to die and be buried with dignity, they lifted up fallen fighters like Veronica Dorsey. They honored leaders like Emanuel McCray, Anthony Williams, and other family and community members who had been buried in the state of Maryland's Potter's Field because they could not afford a proper burial. This day of collective mourning was a reminder that we live in a country where more than two hundred and fifty thousand people die every year because of poverty. As people shared stories of loved ones they had lost, the community gathered to lift up their leadership, insights, and unrelenting commitment to end poverty and the war on the poor.

Mourning, as a celebration of leadership, sustains movements and reminds leaders that they come from and are connected to a long tradition of freedom fighters. While "the least of these" are often passed by and forgotten, moral stand bearers, biblical prophets, and leaders like Veronica Dorsey remind us that God stands on the side of the poor and dispossessed. God lifts up the least of these as leaders in a movement to speak truth to power and build God's kingdom here on earth.

A EULOGY: THE RITUAL

Veronica Dorsey passed away on November 2, 2013. This eulogy was offered by Ashley Hufnagel, a fellow leader at United Workers, at her funeral, which was held on November 7, 2013.

Good morning. My name is Ashley Hufnagel, and it's an incredible honor to stand up here today and pay tribute to Veronica on behalf of the United Workers.

To her family and friends, she might have been known as "Sweetpea," but let's be honest: this nickname is a little deceiving. Anyone who spent even a few moments with her knew Veronica was a force: passionate, committed, smart, and downright funny. She wasn't just "Sweetpea"; she was a powerful leader in the fight for human dignity and freedom from poverty. Veronica first became involved with the United Workers in 2007 when she worked as a cleaner down at Camden Yards. We were at the tail end of a campaign to win living wages for the cleaners at the stadium, and she jumped on board.

She used to like to tell the story about her first United Workers protest. She called off sick from work so she could protest outside the stadium. When her manager saw her, he said, "Hey Veronica, I thought you were sick," to which she replied, "I *am* sick; I'm sick and tired of being treated like trash." This was classic Veronica. She was a powerful communicator and incredible storyteller. It was in this capacity that I had the amazing experience of working with Veronica as part of the communications team. We crafted presentations, speeches, and media events.

So it felt appropriate and special to sit down and write a speech about her. Her stories were able to connect with people on a personal, emotional, intellectual, and spiritual level. This ability to connect and communicate was not just about compelling speeches, it was about relationships. She connected with all sorts of people, cutting across every conceivable line of division: race, gender, language, age, you name it. I vividly remember being in meetings of low-wage workers, Black, White and Latino, going around introducing ourselves, and Veronica would say, 'Hola, me llamo Veronica. Soy un miembro del comite de liderazgo. Hello, my name is Veronica and I am a member of the Leadership Committee.' It wasn't always graceful, and it might seem like a small gesture, but it was an important message of unity she was sending. Janice has already testified to this, but she really did encourage so many to get involved, speak truth to power, and engage in the organizing process. She was a teacher, passing on the knowledge and experience she had gained through the movement.

We are so grateful for all that she has given to the United Workers and the movement to end poverty. We wouldn't be who we are without her.

A BELL CEREMONY: THE RITUAL

This bell ceremony was offered at the United Workers Right to Health memorial and campaign launch that took place in Sykesville, Maryland, on Memorial Day 2024. United Workers members, faith leaders, and loved ones of those who died from poverty marked the launch of the UW Right to Health campaign. The memorial was held near Springfield Hospital, the site of Maryland's Potter's Field, to honor and remember those fallen soldiers in the war on the poor. Leaders came together from across the state of Maryland and across the region to call out the immorality of poverty in one of the richest states in the richest country in the world. The bell ceremony offered during the memorial was an adaptation of one used by leaders of Open Table in Nashville.

For centuries, the ringing of a bell has been used to mark the passing of loved ones. Today, we began our service by remembering those fallen soldiers in the war on the poor—family, friends, and comrades who suffered and died in poverty, some who have been laid to rest in this potter's field, nameless and invisible. But they are not nameless and invisible. We remember them. As we mourn their loss, let their memory be a call to action, a call for life not death. We will ring the bell three times: first, to pause and remember the fallen; second, to honor those who mourn; and third, to guide and inspire us as we carry forth the light of justice. Let us be still and silent as the sound of the bell resonates within us. May we feel it chiming in our hearts and settling down into our bones. Let us remember what was, what is, and what will be.

For all of our friends, family members, and loved ones who have passed from this life. For all who have come before us. For all of their struggle, courage and pain. For all that was.

[*Ring bell and pause until it is silent.*]

For everyone gathered here today. For those who are with us in spirit, far and near. For our friends, family, and loved ones. We laugh together, cry together, sing together, and cling to each other. For the time we still have together. For the present moment and the hopes and dreams it holds. For all that is.

[*Ring bell and pause until it is silent.*]

For our best selves, yet to be. For our friends, family, and all who join us in our quest for justice and an end to poverty amidst plenty. For the light of truth that guides our way. For those who will outlive us and the generations yet to be born. For the coming of a new and better world. For all that will be.

[*Ring bell and pause until it is silent.*]

And so, with the ringing of these bells, we remember, we honor, and we look to the future we will build together. Blessed be.

REFLECT, EMBODY, DISCUSS

1. Consider Veronica's role as a mentor and leadership organizer. How can the lessons from her leadership and activism be applied to your own life or community?
2. What does Ashley's eulogy teach us about the relationship between mourning and celebration? Why is it important to celebrate the leadership of poor and dispossessed people who have fought for change?
3. How does the act of remembering those who have suffered and died in poverty shape our responsibility to act in the present? How can this bell ringing ceremony guide us in creating a future where no one is forgotten or left behind?

MOURNER'S KADDISH AND PRAYER: THE STORY

The Nonviolent Medicaid Army, launched in 2020, is a grassroots network committed to addressing one of the most pressing issues in contemporary American society: health care. This nonviolent army of the poor is fighting for health care as a human right.

The NVMA's efforts echo the work of historical leaders like Jesus, who had the most powerful health care ministry in history and never charged anyone a copay. By focusing on Medicaid for all and the right to health in a broad sense, the NVMA calls for the decommodification of the health care system in the United States and aims to fundamentally transform society, advocating for a system where the health and well-being of every individual is prioritized over profit.

The NVMA identifies health care as a critical issue that has the potential to unite the working class, which is often divided and disorganized. Echoing the words of Martin Luther King Jr., the NVMA believes that millions of people with little to lose, if united, can become a powerful force for change. Health care thus becomes both a unifying strategy for the working class and a vulnerability for the ruling class, which profits heavily from the health care sector.

The health care crisis serves as a tangible basis for uniting the working class. The widespread Medicaid cuts affect individuals in every city, town, and rural area across the United States. It was in organizing to connect with the millions of everyday people who are on or excluded from Medicaid and are impacted by multiple struggles—be it the fight for housing, a healthy environment, living wages, food, education, freedom from debt, freedom of migration, or freedom from criminalization and incarceration—that leaders from the NVMA met Erro Lynd and Julia Willis.

Erro and Julia first got involved with Put People First! PA, an organization that helped launch the NVMA, in 2016. Both had been labor organizers and social justice advocates for years. It had been several years since Erro was diagnosed with leukemia due to ongoing cancer treatment for neuroblastoma, and Julia was facing her own yet-to-be-diagnosed health challenges. They agreed to join PPF-PA to testify at a Pennsylvania Insurance Department hearing. The power of this experience moved Erro and Julia to become active members in PPF-PA.

While Erro and Julia had been part of other organizing efforts in the past, they found a genuine home in the PPF-PA and NVMA community. As they struggled to deal with one health crisis after another and navigate the brutality of a for-profit health care system that treats poor people, disabled people, and sick people as disposable, Erro and Julia found a community that affirmed their commitment to fighting for the health and well-being of all people.

After moving to Wyoming in 2018, Erro and Julio continued to commit their lives to social justice. In 2020, when the NVMA was formed, they began working with this national network to build a NVMA in Wyoming. The deep relationships built among leaders of the NVMA and the commitment to build a society that puts people over profits, did not stop with a legislative campaign to achieve universal health care for all. The power of the community built in the NVMA was exemplified when Erro and Julia's health issues intensified. When traveling to New York to receive cancer treatments, leaders in the NVMA network would connect with Erro and Julia in New York and Philadelphia, building a community of care around them. And in the last days before Erro died, a delegation of thirteen NVMA leaders traveled to Wyoming to help care for Erro and Julia, as Julia's own health was also failing.

This commitment to caring for the lives of our people and being fully present in this struggle for justice even in the darkest of times was illuminated during a Longest Night of the Year Memorial Service and NVMA Art & Culture Night, dedicated to Erro and Julia. Leaders gathered to celebrate their lives and contributions through songs, stories, poetry, and artwork. This virtual gathering was held in December 2023, just days before Erro passed away. It was a coming together of NVMA leaders as well as other friends and family to affirm that we are here for one another and that no one should die alone.

As leaders committed to the work of building a movement to end poverty and injustice across the world, NVMA honored Erro by committing their own lives to continuing the struggle. Zevi, a leader from Put People First! PA said "No one leaves us. Especially people who love the people and love our movement so much—they are always here." This was a sentiment echoed throughout the evening. "It is not shameful or wallowing to feel and remember and mourn our dead loved ones and everyone and everything we've lost along the way," Julia said.

"It is necessary, it is lifesaving, and it is movement sustaining. We're not going to be silent anymore."

Julia emphasized the power of the NVMA's vision and the belief that it is possible to create a world where everyone has what they need. The community gathering affirmed that this is the world we can build together. And this is the world they would continue to fight for.

As Julia poignantly stated, "Life is not separate from this fight, this fight is life. . . . For Erro, when they've passed on to another realm, they're going to be in this fight always. Because they are a part of me, they are a part of all of you." Erro's memory and commitment to the cause live on through the NVMA and its ongoing battle for a just and equitable world.

In January 2024, the NVMA launched their annual winter study and dedicated the course, meant to deepen the consciousness and commitment of their leaders, to Erro Lynd. Nijmie Dzurinko, a founding leader of PPF! PA and the NVMA, opened the course by reaffirming NVMA members' commitment to "embody Erro's vision, Erro's commitment to our class. To building the unity of the poor and dispossessed across all lines of division, to the political independence of our class, and to base building and building the Nonviolent Medicaid Army in new regions."

The NVMA lifts up the importance of honoring the leaders of the poor and dispossessed and it is up to organizations of the poor and dispossessed to write the people's history and to lift up heroes and unsung saints of the people: like Erro Lynd, like Peg Franzen of the Vermont Workers' Center, like Patrick Braswell of the Rochester Homeless Union, and like James Shearer of the Massachusetts Homeless Union.

At several gatherings in 2024, Rebecca Schuchat, a leader with the Vermont Workers' Center, lifted up a traditional Jewish prayer that members of the Freedom Shul of the Poor have been reclaiming—the Mourner's Kaddish—to honor Erro. Rebecca shared that the Mourner's Kaddish is a prayer offered in the Jewish community when someone dies. She explained that while the Mourner's Kaddish is said when someone passes away, there is no mention of death in the prayer itself. Instead, this prayer reminds us that we are called to establish God's kingdom here on earth, to end poverty. The Mourner's Kaddish tells us that this is how we sanctify the dead and honor their memory: by working to create a world without poverty.

As leaders gathered to honor Erro's life, they committed themselves to building a world free from slavery, bondage, poverty, and debt. Rebecca shared that in the Jewish tradition the community says, "May their memory be a blessing," a practice that the movement has embraced, evolving it into "May their memory be a revolution" to honor those who fought and died in the struggle. In this spirit, Briann Moye, a leader of PPF! PA and the NVMA, rewrote the lyrics to the civil rights anthem "We Are Soldiers in the Army," celebrating Erro Lynd as a freedom fighter. Erro, a dedicated leader in the Nonviolent Medicaid Army, fought for the life and dignity of all to the very end. 🌐

MOURNER'S KADDISH AND PRAYER: THE RITUAL

Erro Lynd was a leader in Put People First! PA and the Wyoming Nonviolent Medicaid Army. They battled cancer for two decades and died on December 25, 2023. The prayers shared here were part of a series of memorials and dedications offered to lift up Erro's life and memory among the Nonviolent Medicaid Army and the Freedom Church of the Poor communities.

MOURNER'S KADDISH

The Mourner's Kaddish was offered at the opening session of the NVMA Winter Study and the Freedom Church of the Poor service led by members of the Nonviolent Medicaid Army. Rebecca Schuchat, a leader with the Vermont Workers' Center, offered this prayer in honor of Erro. Rebecca shared that the Mourner's Kaddish is a reminder that when someone dies, what we are called to do is establish God's kingdom here on earth, to end poverty. The Kaddish tells us that this is how we sanctify the dead and honor their memory, by working to create a world without poverty.

Mourner's Kaddish 🌐

Glorified and sanctified be God's great name throughout the world which God has created according to Their will.

May God establish God's kingdom in your lifetime and during your days, and within the life of the entire House of Israel, speedily and soon; and say, Amen.

May God's great name be blessed forever and to all eternity.

Blessed and praised, glorified and exalted, extolled and honored, adored and lauded be the name of the Holy One, blessed be God, beyond all the blessings and hymns, praises and consolations that are ever spoken in the world; and say, Amen.

May there be abundant peace from heaven, and life, for us and for all Israel; and say, Amen.

God who creates peace in God's celestial heights,
may God create peace for us and for all Israel;
and say, Amen.

A PRAYER FOR THOSE WHO HAVE PASSED

In April of 2023 a delegation of leaders from the NVMA traveled to meet with movement leaders in Cuba, to share lessons of organizing and discuss the challenges of fighting for the right to health care. Erro had also spent time in Cuba during college, an experience that contributed to their lifelong commitment to justice work. Members of the delegation gathered during their time in Cuba at El Malecón, to lift up Erro's life and memory and to commit themselves to carrying on Erro's values and legacy. Moses Hernandez McGavin offered a prayer. Here is just a portion of that prayer. The original prayer can be found here. 🌐

Let us begin by saying the names of ancestors out loud—to bring them into the space. They are with us. [*Lift up the names of movement leaders and loved ones who have passed on.*]

Heavenly Spirit, we ask you right now to hear our tears and to hear our pain. We ask you to hear the cry of people for a better life, for a better system, and for better care for each other.

We ask you to hear our wailing as we call the names of those who have died far too soon. We also ask that you present yourself in each and every one of us. In these times when we name those who have left, in times when we are hurting because those that we love the most have gone from this world too soon:

Remind us that you are always with us. Remind us that you are always by our side and that every single one of us is cared for and loved and valued, despite a system that might tell us otherwise. We ask you to be in each and every one of us, that we may show every single other person around us that they are cared for, loved, and valued. Part of what we do on this earth is fight for a system to know that we are all loved. Help us have faith, and help us have hope that these things are possible, and help us see through these times of legitimate pain and crisis and suffering: There is another way, and we have each other. We have each other's love and support and solidarity.

And today, especially, we ask a special prayer and a special blessing for our dear comrades. [*Add some reflections about the lives and commitments of those who have died.*]

Let them feel loved and cared for here. Let them know that we will carry on their legacy, and that we will fight for a revolution, and that we will fight for a just system.

And may every single person that we named—wherever they are right now—all do a big group hug, a big hug of solidarity with each other, so they can all connect through us to know that they are also loved by everyone here. Amen.

REFLECT, EMBODY, DISCUSS

1. How does the idea of health care as a human right align with your ethical and moral beliefs? Reflect on the comparison made between Jesus's ministry and the NVMA's mission. How does this analogy influence your perception of health care access?
2. What are the societal benefits of viewing health care as a fundamental right rather than a commodity? How do you think universal health care could transform society and address systemic inequalities?
3. How has the story of Erro Lynd and Julia Willis affected your view on the power of grassroots activism? What steps can you take to foster a supportive community that sustains your involvement and commitment to this cause over time?

CHAPTER FOUR

TAKING ACTION TOGETHER

As our society continues to be engulfed by crises, the time for complacency has passed. From the lack of health care coverage for tens of millions of Americans to the tragic death toll of endless wars and environmental disasters; from the assault on democracy to the glaring inequalities laid bare by the pandemic, it is clear we stand at a generational crossroads. This is a kairos moment—a time of crisis and opportunity. In biblical terms, it is a moment when the foundations of injustice are exposed, prophetic voices call for change, and movements for justice take root.

Luke 4:14–30 is known as Jesus's first sermon, delivered in his hometown of Nazareth. It marks the beginning of his public ministry during a kairos moment not unlike our own. In his Sermon on the Mount, Jesus announces his mission of societal transformation. He proclaims: "The Spirit of the Lord is upon me, because he has anointed me to bring good news to the poor. He has sent me to proclaim release to the captives and recovery of sight to the blind, to set free those who are oppressed, to proclaim the year of the Lord's favor," (Luke 4:18–19 NIV).

Too often, the Bible's good news is reduced to matters of individual salvation and detached from Jesus's goal to transform the world. But a close reading of the Bible, including the teachings of Jesus, reveals a vast antipoverty program and social justice mission, which call on us to resist unjust economic practices and build a society in which everyone's needs are met.

Drawing strength from these biblical principles, the Freedom Church of the Poor tradition teaches us to stand up for one another, care for the least of these, and dismantle laws that perpetuate injustice.

If we believe that God stands with the oppressed and that Jesus preached liberation, then collective action by those most impacted by injustice is imperative. By taking collective action with and as poor and dispossessed people, we bridge our spiritual convictions and our hunger for transformative change.

As Dr. Martin Luther King Jr. prepared to launch the Poor People's Campaign during another kairos moment in 1967, he emphasized the need for unified action among poor and dispossessed people:

> The dispossessed of this nation—the poor, both white and Negro—live in a cruelly unjust society. They must organize a revolution against that injustice, not against the lives of the persons who are their fellow citizens, but against the structures through which society is refusing to take means which have been called for, and which are at hand, to lift the load of poverty. The only real revolutionary, people say, is a man who has nothing to lose. There are millions of poor people in this country who have very little, or even nothing, to lose. If they can be helped to take action together, they will do so with a freedom and a power that will be a new and unsettling force in our complacent national life.

We are still living in a "cruelly unjust" society, one in which unprecedented wealth and power at the top of our society is maintained through the exploitation and unnecessary death of those at the bottom. Because the poor have the least to lose and the most to gain from transformative change, they could become the new and unsettling force we need to lead all of society toward a moral revolution of values. But this will only happen if the poor are organized to take action together—and as leaders in the movement. The Freedom Church of the Poor tradition rejects the notion that poor people are either criminals or charity cases. Instead, it celebrates poor people as agents of change who are capable of moving our society toward God's vision of justice.

In this chapter we explore the power of collective action—the bonds forged, lives changed, and systems transformed when we pursue justice together. Through a number of stories and reflections, we offer a glimpse of the beauty and the power that emerges from rituals of collective action by the poor.

Storytelling for a Living Wage: Movements begin with the telling of untold stories. In 2023, Jojo Dickson, a Waffle House server from Georgia, shared her story through a poem titled "Her Name is Poverty" while fighting for living wages with the Union of Southern Service Workers (USSW). In a society saturated with misinformation and polarizing narratives, personal testimonies can begin building the collective power we need to abolish poverty and its interlocking injustices. Storytelling is a transformative practice of the Freedom Church community; it allows our communities to become catalysts for collective empowerment. Storytelling breaks the isolation and shame that so often accompanies poverty and helps counter individualized explanations that blame us for our suffering. When we shape and share our own narratives, we offer undeniable evidence of the power poor and dispossessed people can build when we are organized to act together. To shift the narratives around poverty and injustice, we need to shift the narrators.

A Ceasefire Pray-In: Prayer takes many forms. In the Freedom Church tradition, collective action is a holy act of prayer. This section takes us into the halls of Congress and follows the story of forty diverse faith and community leaders, including Muslim, Jewish, and Christian clergy, who joined in prayer to urge New York congressman and Minority Leader of the House of Representatives Hakeem Jeffries to call for an immediate ceasefire in Gaza. When we "pray with our feet," as Rabbi Abraham Joshua Heschel once said, prayer is not confined to the solitude of our hearts but extends onto the streets and into the halls of power. Praying with our feet encapsulates the essence of collective prayer within the context of social justice movements. It moves spiritual conviction into tangible action.

A Project of Survival: When we take action together to serve and advocate for our communities, the fight, plight, and insight of the poor intersect with the divine call for justice. One way to make our collective power tangible is through "projects of survival," like the one from Maine described in this section. Projects of survival are grassroots initiatives that allow poor people to offer one another mutual support and enable their communities to engage in movement building. These projects emanate from activities people undertake to survive, which can then be politicized and organized on a mass level. Projects of survival often arise from existing programs designed to meet people's basic needs, including food distribution programs, medical clinics, housing initiatives, and mutual aid projects. By organizing around these initiatives, we not only address immediate needs but also lay the groundwork for broader social change.

Prayer for Migrant Justice: Howard Zinn once lamented that "our problem [as a society] is civil obedience." He was concerned with the alarming level of societal tolerance and acquiescence to systemic violence in the form of poverty, racism, war, and more. Perhaps unknowingly, Zinn was echoing the words of the prophet Isaiah, who warns, "Woe to those who call evil good and good evil, who put darkness for light and light for darkness" (Isaiah 5:20 NIV). Our task in the Freedom Church tradition is to do whatever we can to help break the cycle of obedience to injustice. In a world where injustice is not only prevalent but often legally sanctioned, nonviolent, moral direct action is a moral imperative. This method of resistance, chronicled here through a multi-faith-led action on the southern border of the United States, is rooted in principles of love and peace, with the goal of effecting wide social, political, and economic change.

Vigil for the Detained: Collective action is not a singular moment but an ongoing practice, one that is strengthened through its connection to the history of struggle by our ancestors. The ritual in this section comes from a series of monthly vigils organized outside a federal prison in New York City to protest the inhumane treatment of detainees held in solitary confinement for extended periods without trial. When we take action together, we are never alone; we call upon the collective strength and support of our communities and the many freedom fighters who came before us. This unity is crucial for sustaining long-term movements.

In the Freedom Church of the Poor tradition, we envision a world where every life is sacred and every need is met. This vision challenges the normalization of injustice and the valuing of profit over people. Through nonviolent, moral direct action—marches, boycotts, sit-ins, and more—we reject the status quo and reclaim the moral narrative. We create spaces where justice is reimagined and a moral revolution of values becomes irresistible.

STORYTELLING FOR A LIVING WAGE: THE STORY

In 2022, low-wage workers across the South came together to form a union. First known as Raise Up the South, the Union of Southern Service Workers emerged as the southern wing of the Fight for $15 movement. The USSW recognizes that their fight goes beyond the injustices of any single employer, aiming to unite workers across the service industry. Historically, workers in the South, particularly Black and Brown workers, have been excluded from union rights, making their struggle especially challenging. Yet members of the USSW understand the power they can build when workers join forces.

One such member is Joanna (JoJo) Dickson, who joined the USSW in 2023. As a low-wage worker living in Georgia and struggling to make ends meet, JoJo had often felt the shame imposed upon poor and low-income people. Feeling lost amid life's challenges, she asked God to show her a purpose for her life. Life has not been easy for JoJo. Growing up in the harsh reality of foster care, she faced abusive relationships and homelessness. In 2023, while working as a Waffle House server, JoJo met USSW leaders who were organizing workers to fight for living wages, workplace safety, and the right to organize. This community became the answer to her prayers, giving her purpose and strength.

Before joining the union, JoJo, like so many poor and low-income people, felt her voice didn't matter. She had never spoken out at her job or engaged with government representatives. The 2024 election marked the first time she voted, which was a significant step, as she had always felt her vote didn't matter. The USSW showed her that by coming together with other impacted people, she had the power not only to stand up for herself but also to take a stand and do what's right for others.

In December 2023, JoJo participated in an action at the Waffle House corporate offices, delivering a petition signed by over thirteen thousand workers and community members demanding workplace safety, twenty-five dollars an hour for all workers, and an end to unfair wage deductions. During this action, JoJo read her poetry aloud for the first time, finding her voice in the movement.

There is a saying in the Freedom Church tradition that "movements begin with the telling of untold stories." When we take action together, we center the stories of those most impacted by injustice. JoJo's story, expressed through poetry, became an invitation to other poor and working people to claim their stories, question why poverty exists, and reject the shame society places on them. In a country where the stigmas around poverty lead people to hide their struggles, JoJo's poetry offers a glimpse into her own plight and calls others to unite and fight.

JoJo's story echoes the questions raised by Rev. Dr. Martin Luther King Jr.: "There are forty million poor people here. And one day we must ask the question, 'Why are there forty million poor people in America?' And when you begin to ask that question, you are raising questions about the economic system, about a broader distribution of wealth. When you ask that question, you begin to question the capitalistic economy. And I'm simply saying that more and more, we've got to begin to ask questions about the whole society."

In coming together with other leaders of the USSW to take action together, JoJo's poetry became more than just words on a page or her own personal reflection; it became a rallying cry for justice and equality. Her storytelling challenges the stigma surrounding poverty and encourages all of us to join the fight for a just society.

STORYTELLING FOR A LIVING WAGE: THE POEM

Poetry for JoJo Dickson has always been an important personal outlet. Writing had helped her heal from pain. But sharing her poetry with others brought forth a new sense of strength and power. Here is the poem she shared at the December 2023 action at the corporate headquarters of Waffle House, demanding workplace safety protocols and a living wage.

"Her Name Is Poverty"

Her name is poverty

You asked me what it means.
What does what mean?
Poverty . . .
Webster defines poverty as such:
The state of One who lacks a usual
or socially acceptable amount of money or materialistic possessions.

But,

To feel or live poverty
From torn and ratted clothes to boiling water for a bath.
Shoes with soles detached
Matted hair, Maybe it smells, Kids bumping, Pushing, Pointing fingers laughing . . .

Laugh

Poverty . . . 12.4 percent of America live in poverty.
That's 38 million, Just plain civilians.

From women with menses that aren't properly cleansed.
Children robbing to bring back cash for food.

Gang bangers organizing together like Nipsey.
Because it's not about the red or the blue.

When you feel, Or you know my quiet, Sucks Friend Poverty . . .

Sometimes it can cause you to lose yourself.
Digging your way out of this never-ending hole.

Her name is poverty

She comes to strip you of your dignity,
Hoping you won't react or fight back

Hungry, Thirsting for knowledge
Believe me when I say
Stay in school.
Don't drop out

The world is a selfish place

When are we going to take a stand like Dr. Martin Luther King?

His dream, Our vision.
We have to make a decision

The wealthy takes care of the rich
Oh Poor, pitiful, poverty party

I pray, God wakes the congregation soon

Those Rose-colored glasses only cover so much
Remove the veil so I may clear

To all my people, white, brown, pink, and purple

Can we come together to change forever?
Forever end poverty

Forever end our children looked at differently
because they Can't afford the latest brand phase

The only way to forever ending the poverty crisis, like Isis

Meet me at the pavilion I'll tell you all about it

How we come together to fight the task at hand

Praying, organizing, unionizing

We as humans need to stick together, always watch each other's
backs

Let's start a revolution

Beautiful families and faces
Multitude of progress

Let's not regenerate
it's lucrative, We organize and come up with a strategy plan to end . . .

Her name is poverty.

REFLECT, EMBODY, DISCUSS

1. Get a piece of paper and map out your own life. Where and how have you encountered poverty? What conditions existed around you that allowed poverty to exist? How did you and others respond?
2. In a society that blames people for their poverty, JoJo invites us to walk a mile in her shoes. Do you see yourself in JoJo's story? Can you recognize or empathize with the challenges she has faced?
3. How does JoJo's journey inspire you? What ways can you connect with others who are standing up and saying, "No more will we accept poverty and the way it strips us of our humanity and our dignity?" How can you come together with others in your community to end the injustice of poverty?

A CEASEFIRE PRAY-IN: THE STORY

In the wake of devastating Israeli bombing and the tragic loss of Palestinian lives, and following the brutal Hamas attacks on October 7, 2023, a group of forty diverse faith and community leaders came together in the office of House Minority Leader Hakeem Jeffries to call for an immediate ceasefire in Gaza. They came with an understanding that the conflict between Israel and Palestine did not begin on October 7 but that this was a deeply entrenched struggle that spanned decades. They knew the conflict was marked by sorrow, violence, and an ignored history of Israeli occupation and apartheid in the region.

The coalition understood that silence and inaction were no longer options. Led by Adalah Justice Project, US Campaign for Palestinian Rights, Jewish Voice for Peace, Dream Defenders, Rising Majority, and the Kairos Center for Religions, Rights, and Social Justice, the group came together with a single message: "Ceasefire is the only moral choice, and the world is watching your next move." This slogan was introduced by Palestinian organizer Sandra Tamari of the Adalah Justice Project as she urged faith leaders—in particular Christian leaders, who had not yet been organizing en masse—to speak out against the American government's support for Israel in carrying out mass atrocities in Gaza.

The decision to hold a pray-in on October 24 at Representative Jeffries's office was strategic. It followed a major rally and march in Washington, DC, organized by the Rising Majority, which demanded that President Biden and Congress uphold the value of all human life by working to de-escalate the violence. The pray-in aimed to put forward a moral appeal directly to Representative Jeffries to do the right thing, to stand courageously, and call for an immediate ceasefire, an end to genocide, and a free Palestine.

During the pray-in, the leaders solemnly remembered the innocent Palestinians who had perished in the violence. Rabbi Alissa Wise of Rabbis for Ceasefire passionately pleaded with Jeffries's staff, emphasizing the urgency of the situation and the moral imperative to act: "Over two thousand children [at that time] have been killed. And it's being done in the name of the Jewish people. And the message of Judaism is one of life. The most sacred obligation in Jewish tradition is *pikuach nefesh*, which is 'saving a life.' It trumps every other law."

Palestinian leaders present shared the names and ages of those killed by the Israeli assault, including infants like Hamed, only forty days old. Each name read aloud was a stark reminder of the human cost of war and the urgency of a permanent ceasefire. Mirrors bearing the words "The world is watching" were raised, urging congressional leaders and staff to reflect on their role in perpetuating the cycle of violence.

In an act of solidarity and defiance, the leaders occupied Rep. Jeffries's office as moral standard bearers. They sang songs of resistance, including "Courage," a song that originated in the South African anti-apartheid struggle, as a petition for courage to stop funding militarism and instead invest in life.

This collective action served as a rallying cry for justice and a call to build a world free from racism, ethnic cleansing, and state violence. The pray-in at Rep. Jeffries's office was not just a plea for ceasefire; it was a powerful statement of resistance and solidarity. It highlighted the moral imperative to act and the urgent need to end the suffering of the Palestinian people. The world indeed was watching, and it was time for leaders to heed the call of conscience.

A CEASEFIRE PRAY-IN: THE PRAYER AND SONG

This prayer was written and delivered by minister Jessica Anderson at the Ceasefire Pray-In at Rep. Hakeem Jeffries's office on Tuesday, October 24, 2023.

PRAYER

O liberating God, the world is watching. Make us resolute that there is nothing more righteous than to love you and love our neighbor. God, remind us that we have your solidarity and your witness. Thank you that you have joined all of us to the genealogy of people who have pushed for justice before us. Guide us, through the inspiration of our sacred texts and sacred reminders, so that when we get tired of standing for justice, we stand, nevertheless. Nothing should separate us from the love of our God. Not trouble, not persecution, not famine, not swords, not governments, not Twitter bans, not wicked theologies, not misinformation, not weariness from yet another fight for justice.

Remind us that you hear us when we ask, How long? How long shall blood cry out from the ground? How long will political leaders hear "Where is your Palestinian brother?" and ask, "Am I my brother's keeper?" How long shall our faith be co-opted to defend wickedness from high places?

O misunderstood God, remind us that the elders say you walk with us and talk with us, but you also march with us and sit with us.

O God of peace, hear our prayers. Move us to DC—Ceasefire now!—and strengthen our hearts toward justice. Amen.

SONG

This song, "Courage," was adapted from a South African anti-apartheid movement song. Protesters sang it as they were being taken to jail and as a way to learn people's names in the jail cells. This song has special significance to the liberation struggle in Palestine, as a song connecting with communities around the world who have fought against apartheid. 🌐

Courage, my friend
You do not move alone
We will move with you
And sing your spirit home

REFLECT, EMBODY, DISCUSS

1. In times of crisis and conflict, what responsibilities do faith communities have in advocating for peace and justice? How can religious leaders and individuals use their platforms to effect meaningful change? How do moments like these challenge us all to recognize the vision for justice that is foundational to our faith traditions?
2. How does the story challenge conventional notions of prayer as a private, internal practice? What does it mean to "pray with our feet"—and how does this concept reshape our understanding of prayer as a tool for social change? How does this concept of prayer also reshape our vision for what protest and social action look like?
3. Explore the use of language and rituals, such as prayers and songs, in social justice movements. How do these elements contribute to the mobilization of participants and the creation of collective meaning?

A PROJECT OF SURVIVAL: THE STORY

In the heart of a community, a prayer emerges—not from traditional places of worship, but from the streets where the plight and fight of poor and dispossessed people intersect with the divine call for justice.

Katie Vandersall Thiesen, a leader with the Poor People's Campaign in Maine, was raised in traditional church settings: attending Sunday services, going to youth group, and singing in the choir. There were coffee hours and brunches, garage sales and talent shows. But when her husband, Adam, was diagnosed with epilepsy, their family faced thousands of dollars in medical bills, despite having health insurance through the Affordable Care Act. As their access to medical care became a matter of life and death, they realized that God's justice would be realized through a movement of people fighting for social change. Their faith found new meaning in a movement.

Katie's commitment to the Poor People's Campaign grew as she became more involved in the struggles of people living on the streets and saw the disparities confronting those facing homelessness in Maine. She began to question the nature of church in the face of these crises, asking, "What is church—and what ought church be?"

In October 2020, her town faced a growing housing crisis, with six times more homeless people than the previous year. Rather than securing additional housing, however, the local government responded by cracking down on homeless encampments. When police destroyed a local tent encampment, a diverse group—including the unhoused, formerly homeless, and housing advocates—came together to take a stand.

They returned to the park where the encampment had been, slept out in tents, and held a community meeting. This gathering evolved into weekly meetings at a nearby bus stop, where, despite blizzards and barricades, a makeshift congregation came together—not for scripted prayers but to share meals and stories, and to organize.

The community grew, as leaders reached out to more and more people in the neighborhood. They organized around the basic survival needs that existed for unhoused leaders in their community. As their numbers grew, they won demands from the city council—like public restrooms in a town that had none. But their victories and their defeats were just the beginning of a nonviolent battle. Convincing people that no one should be homeless in a country of such abundance, was a long-term struggle.

Katie remembers the leaders from the streets writing a collective letter to established religious communities, asking them to join the movement. Yet even her own church met the letter with silence, multiple times. The prayers offered for the poor in her congregation suddenly seemed hollow, and while Katie found a deep sense of community and solidarity in the streets, she felt pain and silence within the walls of her church.

In the face of these contradictions, Katie asked God to help her unlearn what humans had made church to be. This marked a turning point, a departure from the comfort of familiarity toward the discomfort of transformation. While she hadn't been taught that church included organizing at bus stops, she realized that showing up there could be her new ritual, her new church. This gathering wasn't just to help people at the bus stop; it was for everyone: those who were unhoused and those who were just one crisis away from joining them. The community became an embodied prayer, a commitment to show up, stand in solidarity, and dismantle systems of oppression that divide and dehumanize.

A PROJECT OF SURVIVAL: A PRAYER AND A SONG

This prayer, written by Katie Vandersall Thiesen, rises out of the story of a community organizing together in the streets. This prayer is also an embodied ritual. You can change the "us" to "me" and the "our" to "my" to make it more personal or to use for solitary prayer.

PRAYER

God, help us see that church was never about buildings nor Sunday morning coffee hours. Your church was always about true worship—and worshipping you means what you share in Amos 5:21–24, Micah 6:6–8 (go back and don't leave out verses 6 and 7!), Isaiah 1:11–17, Matthew 23:23, Acts 4:32, and more.

Worshipping you means actively loving all you love. Worshipping you means nonviolently going directly against the empire that crushes your creation. Worshipping you means restructuring our systems so we can best love one another in a justice-filled society. Worship for you was never focused on the beautiful hymns, nor the fiery sermons, nor any charity that leaves your people in systems where they remain dehumanized. Worshipping you means tirelessly striving for all creation to survive and thrive!

God, help us show up. Help that be our new and forever ritual. What we do after this first ritual of showing up may change. New rituals in our community will grow. But first let our new ritual be showing up in the places of pain that come from injustice. Let me show up willing to, as one organizer said, hold grief in one hand and hope in the other.

A hope that can only come from long-term organizing.

And God, we are afraid. We are afraid of showing up for permanent relationship building in bus stops or seeing our church food pantry or our church meals as places of worship and organizing. We have all been divided for so long that all we know is how to avoid, ignore, or share charity, if we even do that. We are afraid of building a movement to end poverty and all its interlocking injustices. We are afraid because we have never done anything like this before. We are afraid because change is hard. We are fearful because we don't know one another.

> We don't know how it will go.
> What in the world do we say?
> What the heck do we do?

God, keep making us *most* afraid of *not* joining in what you call true worship: Loving all of creation and working for justice together. Keep making us *more* afraid of siblings dying in the streets, of white supremacy having a literal chokehold on our people, of bombs being dropped on children thousands of miles away, of our earth moaning as another creature goes extinct and beyond.

Keep making us *more* afraid of our silence and inaction. Keep making us *more* afraid of the status quo than we are of moving toward a movement of community, love and life itself! Keep reminding us that we do not have to come with, nor do we ever alone have to have all the answers.

Instead, we will come to repeatedly understand and witness our worth and the worth of all of your creation, to learn alongside one another as those of us who are wanting to follow in the way of movement ancestors before us—people who didn't pray in empty words but embodied their prayers by actively organizing to end empire. Keep making our prayer not be empty words.

Instead, make our prayer not be words at all but actually be the ritual of us showing up in spaces like bus stops to build deep relationships and organize for justice. We will not be alone in these places—there is so much life there.

God, make the way we live our lives, the ways that we interact with all of your beloved creation, make joining in the building of your movement of loving justice on earth together, make all this be our ongoing ritual, prayer, and worship of you.

1-2-3 LIFT UP: A SONG

This song was written by Adam Thiesen, a movement leader with the Maine Poor People's Campaign. 🌐

When the people who stand up get in step
Ain't no hill too high for us to climb
Now too few have had too much for too long
I can't think of any worse crime

(Chorus; sing after each verse)
We need people who stand up to get in step
Grab the bottom 1 2 3 and lift up
Lift up and look up to the lowly
Grab the bottom 1 2 3 and lift up

We got churches that feed people to feel good
We got people who got no place to sleep
Who need more than a meal and a handshake
Who need more than a smile that's skin deep

(Chorus)

It's not enough to stand up
We gotta move our feet to move up
Locked arms, lockstep we won't back up
Grab the bottom 1 2 3 and lift up

(Chorus)

REFLECT, EMBODY, DISCUSS

1. How does Katie's journey help you reimagine traditional notions of church and worship? How might Katie's story inspire you to rethink the role of faith and community engagement in your life?
2. Reflect on the role of action in worship, as highlighted in Katie's prayer. How does her prayer emphasize the importance of actively engaging with issues of justice and oppression?
3. In what ways does Adam Thiesen's song "1-2-3 Lift Up" reinforce the themes of collective action and solidarity? How does it complement Katie's prayer in illustrating the embodiment of faith through activism?

PRAYER FOR MIGRANT JUSTICE: THE STORY

In November 2018, amid escalating tensions at the United States-Mexico border, the American Friends Service Committee (AFSC) and the Poor People's Campaign issued a call to clergy across the United

States for mass action at the San Diego-Tijuana border. Under the banner Love Knows No Borders: A Moral Call for Migrant Justice, the initiative responded to the growing militarization of the border and the injustices faced by migrant communities.

In response to caravans of migrants traveling north from Central America, the Trump administration had deployed thousands of military troops to the border, blocking migrants from seeking asylum—a right guaranteed by both international and American law. This led to a humanitarian crisis, with families and children facing violence and repression.

The week of action, held December 10–18, coincided with the seventieth anniversary of International Human Rights Day and International Migrants Day, as well as *Las Posada*, a time when Christians prepare to welcome a family seeking shelter and reflect on how we treat the least among us. Over five hundred faith and community leaders gathered at the San Diego-Tijuana border. Pedro Rios, director of AFSC's U.S./Mexico Border Program, emphasized the escalating violence against migrants, including the tear-gassing of families and attempts to criminalize asylum seekers. Maria Puga, whose husband Anastasio Hernandez Rojas was brutally killed by border agents in 2010, testified to the pain migrant families endure and the lack of accountability: "They act with impunity. . . . There is no transparency, there is no justice." The increase of military troops, National Guard, and Border Patrol further intensified the situation.

Rev. Dr. Beth Johnson, a local faith leader who worked with the San Diego Immigrant Rights Consortium and the Unitarian Universalist Refugee and Immigrant Services and Education (UURISE) at the time, recognized the moral dilemma our country was facing and joined the action. Rev. Johnson first got involved with movement work through the San Diego Interfaith Center for Worker Justice. When she moved to San Diego in 2004, she quickly realized justice for workers and justice for immigrants were intertwined. Listening to migrant workers' stories deepened her commitment to their struggle, and as the migrant crisis escalated in 2018, she felt compelled to act.

On December 10, Human Rights Day, faith leaders of various traditions gathered at the border fence to perform a religious ceremony in solidarity with asylum seekers. The action demanded an end to immigrant detention and deportation, respect for the human right to migrate, and an end to border militarization. It emphasized the moral imperative to recognize the humanity of all individuals, regardless of nationality or legal status.

In the presence of military troops and border guards, and within earshot of those on the Mexican side of the border, the community knelt in prayer, singing songs of love and resistance. Their action was a cry for justice and compassion in the face of cruelty. Despite the risks, they put their bodies on the line to shine a light on the injustice of detention and deportation. As they sang, "love, love, love, love / sisters, brothers, hear our call / we will not bow to injustice / God loves us all," their voices carried across the border, expressing deep solidarity with those who dared to hope. 🌐

For Pedro Rios, Maria Puga, Rev. Johnson, and hundreds of faith and community leaders from across the country who had gathered, this was more than a protest; it was a declaration that everyone deserves the right to live with dignity. Rev. Johnson reflected,

> Love knows no borders. Just like the birds that fly overhead and the ocean that laps the shore—Love knows no borders. As we walked the muddy path and onto the beach from Border Field State Park, with each step, my mind was on the migrants who make an arduous and dangerous exodus to reach safety and asylum. As I knelt inches away from border agents and concertina wire, my mind was on the refugees and on the soulless policies and practices that disregard human dignity. In the world I am working for, people fleeing poverty and violence are welcomed with compassion, warmth, food, hospitality and freedom.

In a society that often criminalizes migrants and enforces borders, the Love Knows No Borders action reminded us of our moral obligation to uphold human rights and dignity for all. Through direct, nonviolent action, faith and community leaders stood against injustice and called for a world where love transcends borders. By embracing solidarity, civil disobedience, and unwavering commitment to love, individuals can create meaningful change and uphold the inherent dignity of every person. Love's calling is universal, transcending boundaries, and it is imperative that we heed its call in our pursuit of justice and compassion.

PRAYER FOR MIGRANT JUSTICE: THE POEM

This prayer-poem, "Love's Calling," was written by Rev. Dr. Beth Johnson and shared as part of the Love Knows No Borders interfaith service of witness.

Love's Calling . . .
Love's calling
  Can you hear it?
Love's calling
  All
    all around

Love's calling . . .
      From the depths of our souls
It emerges
      Love's calling . . .
Stirring
  Longing
    Luring
      Leading
        Hearts
          Beating for justice, beating for hope

Hearts beating
  Pulsing through bodies on the line.

Love's calling
Me
You
Us
Love's calling
beating hearts
bruised and worn-out bodies
Rising spirits
Love's calling
from the streets
from the border . . . from the margins

Love's calling
Whispering
Shouting
Raging
Praying
Love's calling
All
All around
Love's calling
for justice

Love's calling
Igniting courage,
Love's calling us . . .

On this journey, love knows no borders . . . love takes us to the depths of our grief,

to the depths of our longing and to the depths of our souls, love stirs in us with compassion and passion,

love rises into action . . .

love flows through us and among and beyond us to
our siblings in exodus because love knows no
borders . . .

So it is love that calls us here in this time, in this place, for this sacred purpose to prepare our hearts and minds and bodies to be witnesses for love and justice.

REFLECT, EMBODY, DISCUSS

1. The action emphasized the moral imperative to recognize the humanity of all individuals, regardless of nationality or legal status. How does this principle resonate with your own values?
2. Rev. Dr. Beth Johnson felt compelled to take action due to her commitment to justice for workers and immigrants. What personal experiences or beliefs motivate you to engage in social justice causes?
3. In what ways can you contribute to promoting migrant justice and upholding human rights in your own community, drawing inspiration from actions like Love Knows No Borders?

VIGIL FOR THE DETAINED: THE STORY

The post-9/11 era has drastically changed the United States' approach to national security, particularly concerning the treatment of individuals accused of terrorism-related offenses. A stark example of this was the Metropolitan Correctional Center (MCC), a federal prison in lower Manhattan. There, people accused of terrorism-related offenses were held in solitary confinement for years without trial.

On February 10, 2014, the No Separate Justice: A Post-9/11 Domestic Human Rights Campaign launched monthly vigils outside the MCC to protest the inhumane treatment of detainees. The campaign aimed to illuminate and end the human rights and civil liberties abuses prevalent in "war on terror" cases within the American criminal justice system.

Despite the MCC's central location in Manhattan, its harsh conditions remained largely unknown to the public due to strict restrictions on access for human rights monitors and the press. The No Separate Justice campaign aimed to break this silence, raising awareness and advocating for policy changes that respect human rights and civil liberties.

Each month, a dedicated group of community leaders, activists, faith leaders, professors, journalists, family members, and students gathered to protest the unjust national security programs targeting Muslim Americans after 9/11. While American national security programs operated with impunity, these monthly vigils refused to allow the abuses taking place in prisons and courtrooms across the United States to remain invisible.

During the April 2014 vigil, Abu Yousuf, an Islamic scholar and advocate with the Muslim Justice Initiative, emphasized the broader impact of these gatherings: "Bearing witness in front of MCC isn't just for Sadequee and the others [detained] on the inside; the presence of the No Separate Justice campaign makes a difference for people on the outside, too. Vigils like these mitigate the impact [of surveillance and policing]. [They] make it easier for speakers in mosques, in communities, to speak truth to power." This solidarity across various identities and beliefs was a form of collective action, one that rejected the isolation of Muslim community members and gave voice to the injustice happening at the MCC.

Lu Aya, a Bronx-based spoken word artist and member of the Peace Poets, was a regular participant in the monthly vigils. Lu uses music to foster solidarity and resilience in movement spaces. Reflecting on those cold winter vigils, he recalled leaning into the transformative power of music. In a city of eight million, with only a few people gathered, building communal power through music might seem like an insurmountable feat. But as he looked around at the people gathered at vigils and protests like this—people who took time out of their hectic lives to show up for justice—he came to really appreciate others. He began to recognize the tremendous power that this body of people represented. And he realized that people continue to show up because of all the people who taught them to love and struggle for justice. He suggested that every time we go to a vigil, we bring along our ancestors and our teachers, our communities and our comrades.

"We have not come here alone," Lu shared, leading the group singing "Never Alone," a song that has come to be lifted up across various social justice movements, including the Poor People's Campaign: A National Call for Moral Revival. It has been used in climate justice actions, as Indigenous leadership remind us to honor and acknowledge the ancestors. And in Minneapolis, social movement artist Jayanthi Kyle has brought "Never Alone" into community memorials, adapting its message to comfort and unify, with the heart-felt assurance, "You are not going alone."

On that cold April day in 2014, Lu reminded those gathered that "we carry our people in our bones, we have not come here alone, and all we got to do is listen—you can hear them in our soul."

The monthly vigils held by the No Separate Justice campaign created a powerful ritual space that emphasized the power of collective action. Songs served as reminders that participants are supported by a larger community, both present and ancestral. This spiritual strength, rooted in a long tradition of movements for justice, highlighted the importance of cultural and emotional solidarity in sustaining long-term social justice movements. Through the monthly vigils and the involvement of community artists like the Peace Poets, the campaign not only raised awareness but also offered a collective reminder that in the fight for justice, no one stands alone.

VIGIL FOR THE DETAINED: THE SONG

This song was written by the Peace Poets, an artist collective known for their fusion of poetry, hip-hop, and education. Founded on the principles of friendship, community, and creative expression, The Peace Poets have made a significant impact on social movements by revitalizing the art of collective singing in public actions. This song, "Never Alone," is a testament to the group's mission that seeks to transform stages and streets into deeply human gatherings where everyone is encouraged to contribute to a world that honors future generations. 🌐

I have not come here alone
I carry my people in my bones
I have not come here alone
If you listen you can hear them in my soul

REFLECT, EMBODY, DISCUSS

1. What was the significance of monthly vigils in building broader awareness about post-9/11 national security measures in the United States? How did this form of action foster solidarity and resilience in the campaign?
2. Consider the statement by Abu Yousuf regarding the impact of the vigils on both detainees and the wider community. What does this suggest about the power of public protest and communal support in social justice movements?
3. Reflect on the lyrics of the song and its significance in the context of collective action and social movements. How does this idea resonate with other movements you are familiar with?

CHAPTER FIVE

CELEBRATION

In a world that often tells the poor and dispossessed that we are not worthy, celebration is an act of moral revolution. Celebration is a declaration of our inherent right to life; of our right to not merely survive but thrive. In spaces where we lift each other up, we celebrate our leadership, our history of struggle, and our unity. Celebration is an essential strategy for deepening our connections to one another and our collective commitment to create change.

Celebration is a reminder that another world is possible and a call to build that world together. Communal celebration within the Freedom Church of the Poor tradition embraces the diverse experiences and histories that have paved our path toward justice. By lifting up these histories and the wisdom won from hard-fought struggle, we can break down the barriers that have kept us divided. Celebrating who we are and where we come from humanizes us and helps us recognize the sacredness in ourselves and one another.

Music, dance, poetry, and other rituals often accompany communal celebrations, physically connecting us and synchronizing our hearts. This coming together happens on both conscious and unconscious levels. Our hearts, minds, and spirits are moved when we celebrate through creative expression. We become more willing to commit our lives to one another and build a better world in which everyone's needs are met.

In the daily struggle against injustice, communities of the poor and dispossessed are often deprived of celebration. Injustice dehumanizes our people, stripping us of our agency and dignity. Our whole society is in crisis, yet continues to blame poor people for their poverty instead of recognizing the structures that perpetuate it. But, when we come together in celebration, we infuse our communities with the powerful spirit of struggle. We refuse to be silent or forgotten, and we demand a better world.

As we fight against the oppression of our communities and cry out for justice, it's crucial that we draw strength from the victories and lessons of past and present freedom struggles. Throughout history, poor and oppressed communities have time and again united and contributed to transformative and positive societal change. The Freedom Church of the Poor tradition reminds us of these struggles and urges us to continue them today through deep and lasting solidarity.

S'bu Zikode of Abahlali baseMjondolo, the South African shack dwellers' movement, reminds us: "When we are together, the first thing we must do is recognize the humanity of each and every one of us, because it's only from that position of humanity that we can take our place among other people on this earth." We gather to defend our humanity. We celebrate to make the world more human.

Litany for an Anniversary: Celebrations that honor the leadership of poor and dispossessed people bring together diverse voices from interfaith, interspiritual, and nonreligious backgrounds, creating the moral resurrection so desperately needed in these times. The Poverty Initiative, now known as the Kairos Center for Religions, Rights, and Social Justice, has nurtured the development of dozens of poor people's movements and organizations over the last two decades. When the Poverty Initiative celebrated its ten-year anniversary, we developed a litany that celebrated the powerful leadership of poor and dispossessed communities and called for the creation of a more just and equitable world. This litany reminds us how important it is to mark and memorialize the often-unseen work of our communities.

Prayer for Launching a Campaign: Prayer as celebration can mark significant milestones in the life cycles of social movements, both past and present. Movement anniversaries are sacred moments that commemorate the achievements of our ancestors, renew our shared commitments, and compel us to continue the work today. This chapter features a prayer from the launch of the Poor People's Campaign: A

National Call for Moral Revival in 2017, which took up Dr. Martin Luther King Jr.'s unfinished work of uniting people across all lines of division to end poverty, racism, and militarism on the fiftieth anniversary of the 1968 Poor People's Campaign.

Chant of the Ancestors: In a world where Black people must struggle daily against systemic oppression, joy is a powerful act of resistance. The celebration of Black joy serves as both a counternarrative to the pervasive devaluation of Black lives and an intentional praxis for healing, resilience, and community building. Freedom songs and liberation chants, foundational to Black activism, underscore the role of music as a tool for connection and empowerment. Organizations like the Black Youth Project 100 emphasize the importance of rituals and music within the Black radical tradition, reminding all movements for justice that centering joy is a critical political act—one that sustains organizers and offers a vision of the radically different world they strive to create.

Song of Belonging for Community Organizing: In the United States, 140 million people live in poverty or just one crisis away from economic ruin. This section introduces Anu Yadav, an actress, playwright, and cultural organizer who became involved in organizing against displacement from gentrification in Washington, DC. She once thought of herself as an ally rather than someone who was poor—until she got an illegal eviction notice and received support from her community. Her song about belonging reminds us how important it is to break through the mythmaking and isolation that keeps our communities divided and impoverished.

The Freedom Church of the Poor tradition echoes Dr. Martin Luther King Jr.'s proclamation that "Power for poor people will really mean having the ability, the togetherness, the assertiveness, and the aggressiveness to make the power structure of this nation say yes when they may be desirous to say no." The togetherness Dr. King envisioned is not easily achieved; structural and social barriers have been designed to prevent our unity. Yet by celebrating our collective strength and fostering deeper bonds of solidarity, we can overcome these obstacles and work toward a more just and equitable future.

We do not celebrate the existence of poverty, but we must celebrate the power and creativity of the poor and dispossessed people organizing to abolish it. In a time of plenty marred by so much poverty, organizing for social, political, and economic change is holy work.

LITANY FOR A CELEBRATION: THE STORY

In 1999, the history of poor and dispossessed people organizing in the United States merged with Union Theological Seminary's legacy of social justice. As it had done many times before when movements for justice emerged, Union opened its doors to hundreds of poor and homeless families from throughout the United States, Latin America, and Canada, who had marched from Washington, DC, to the United Nations in New York City in the "March of the Americas."

March organizers filed the first legal petition in history charging the United States with violating the Universal Declaration of Human Rights by failing to provide adequate public education, accessible health care, affordable housing, and living-wage jobs. Among the organizers were early Poverty Initiative members, including founders Willie Baptist, Rev. Dr. Liz Theoharis, Dr. Chris Caruso, Dawn Plummer, and Rev. Cathlin Baker, who began envisioning an organization dedicated to ending poverty.

The Poverty Initiative was founded in May 2004 at Union Theological Seminary by students, faculty, staff, and community leaders, drawing from Union's two-hundred-year legacy of social justice ministries and Rev. Dr. Martin Luther King's vision of a poor people's campaign. The initiative aimed to raise generations of religious and community leaders committed to building a movement led by the poor to end poverty.

In its first years, the Poverty Initiative built an extensive network of grassroots and religious leaders through organizing campaigns, immersion courses, truth commissions, and other activities. They helped build and support important poor-people-led organizations like the Coalition of Immokalee Workers, United for Respect, the Vermont Workers'

Center, and United Workers. In 2007, they launched the Poverty Scholars Program, dedicated to studying the root causes of poverty and economic inequality, connecting leaders from over twenty-five states and seventeen countries.

A crucial aspect of the Poverty Initiative's work was its emphasis on religion's role in fighting poverty. Traditional theological frameworks often justify poverty, blame the poor, or reduce them to mere objects of pity. In contrast, the Poverty Initiative developed a lived theology and a radical, inclusive method of biblical interpretation. This approach shifted the focus from blaming the poor and offering charity to following a biblical mandate for ending poverty, emphasizing the leadership of those most impacted by it.

On April 24, 2014, the Poverty Initiative, now known as the Kairos Center for Religions, Rights, and Social Justice, celebrated its ten-year anniversary. For a decade, this organization had nurtured efforts to build a social movement to end poverty led by those most affected by it. As economic conditions worsened, the need to unite the poor across divisions became even more critical. The anniversary celebration became a platform for strategic dialogue, gathering grassroots leaders nationwide to discuss the fiftieth anniversary of Dr. King's Poor People's Campaign and a plan to reignite a poor people's campaign today.

The gathering included diverse leaders from various struggles, united by the belief that poverty is a societal sin. It brought together young people organizing for quality education in Philadelphia; homeless organizers and day laborers advocating for living wages in Baltimore; military veterans opposing the war economy; migrant and domestic workers who were fighting for the rights of excluded workers; religious leaders and seminarians inspired by Dr. King's legacy; and struggling artists and cultural organizers contributing their talents to the movement. They celebrated past victories and set the direction for future organizing efforts, emphasizing the urgent need to build a campaign that unites the poor across all dividing lines.

During the tenth anniversary celebration, Rev. Dr. Jessica Williams and Rev. Vanessa Cardinale, pastors and community organizers leading the movement, shared a litany that highlighted the importance of collective leadership in the fight against poverty. The litany emphasized that the movement was not about any single charismatic leader but about leaders organizing others to fight for freedom from want and human misery. It called on everyone to recognize the power of poor and dispossessed leaders and to continue the struggle for justice, drawing on a biblical mandate to end poverty. This powerful moment of reflection and unity reaffirms the long tradition of freedom fighters and the righteous struggle for justice today.

LITANY FOR A CELEBRATION: THE PRAYER

Note: This litany, "Let Your Light Shine," is adapted from a litany written by Rev. Dr. Jessica Williams and Rev. Vanessa Cardinale for the tenth anniversary of the Poverty Initiative. 🌐

Reader 1: Would you please stand as we join together in a call-and-response? Tonight each time you hear that you are the light of the world, please respond, encouraging those around you, by saying "let your light shine." [Practice once.]

Reader 2: You who build anti-poverty ministries, who seek to move beyond charity toward the biblical mandate of ending poverty: You are the light of the world.

All: Let your light shine.

Reader 1: You who advance the mission of ending poverty and of God's reign on earth: You are the light of the world.

All: Let your light shine.

Reader 2: You that practice radical inclusivity and model theologies of liberation: You are the light of the world.

All: Let your light shine.

Reader 1: You who are leaders dedicated to building a social movement to end poverty led by the poor: You are the light of the world.

All: Let your light shine.

Reader 2: You who carry on the work and the legacy of Rev. Dr. Martin Luther King Jr., Harriet "Moses" Tubman, Veronica Dorsey, Ron Casanova, and other fallen fighters: You are the light of the world.

All: Let your light shine.

Reader 1: You who bear the light of resurrection and the values of a revolution: you are the light of the world.

All: Let your light shine.

Reader 2: You are a new and unsettling force. You are the light of the world.

All: Let your light shine.

Reader 1+ 2: You are the Freedom Church of the Poor. You are the light of the world.

All: Let your light shine.

REFLECT, EMBODY, DISCUSS

1. Take a moment to think about a person in your life who has paved your path toward justice. What inspires you about the way they lived their life? What commitments can you make to honor the path that they paved?
2. Why is it significant to not only commemorate historical movements (like the Poor People's Campaign) but also to make a commitment to continue the work of historical movements?

PRAYER FOR A MOVEMENT ANNIVERSARY: THE STORY

In his final years, Rev. Dr. Martin Luther King Jr. sought to deeply understand the causes and conditions of poverty. Speaking to the Southern Christian Leadership Conference in August 1967, he called for a deeper examination of economic disparities. "There are forty million poor people here," he said. "And one day we must ask the question, 'Why are there forty million poor people in America?' "

King's call to question the very foundations of the economic system moved the focus of his organizing from civil rights to a broader human rights agenda that sought to dismantle the systemic roots of poverty. King recognized that poverty was not merely a consequence of bad policies or personal misfortunes but a product of the existing economic system, which he argued was rooted in capitalism and inherently produced and perpetuated poverty. Therefore, the problem of poverty and the needs and demands of poor people cannot be addressed apart from the problems facing the whole of society.

In his analysis, King described the poor as the "dispossessed," highlighting their lack of ownership and control over economic institutions. This lack of control forced them into a cycle of seeking low-wage jobs to survive, while those who owned these institutions continued to profit. King asserted that the interests of the wealthy capitalists were fundamentally opposed to those of the poor, as maintaining their wealth depended on the exploitation and impoverishment of the dispossessed.

By early 1967, King was convinced that civil rights gains were insufficient without addressing the intertwined threats of racism, poverty, and militarism. To meet its own goals, the civil rights movement would need to shift its target to the elimination of pervasive poverty that was impacting not only poor Blacks but the poor of all races, at home and abroad, including poor whites. He called for a shift from a reform movement to a revolutionary movement that questioned the entire social structure. At a Southern Christian Leadership Conference retreat in May 1967, he proclaimed the need for a broader social movement aimed at ending poverty, led by the poor themselves.

In December 1967, King announced the Poor People's Campaign, a plan to bring poor people from across the country to Washington, DC. This campaign sought to unite the poor across racial, ethnic, and geographic lines, creating a force capable of challenging the nation's consciousness and demanding systemic change.

While building the multiracial leadership of the poor through this campaign, King was assassinated. Less than a month after his death on April 4, 1968, the campaign launched on Mother's Day, May 12, 1968, with a march in Washington, DC, led by Coretta Scott King and mothers in the National Welfare Rights Organization. Resurrection City, an encampment of over six thousand poor people, was constructed on the National Mall and became a hub for the movement. The campaign reached its peak on June 19, 1968, when fifty thousand people joined the residents of Resurrection City for a Solidarity Day rally.

The encampment was forcibly shut down on June 24, 1968, and the movement faced retrenchment as poor people returned to organizing in their local communities. However, the reasons for building a poor people's campaign continued to grow.

Fifty years later, leaders like Dr. Savina Martin, a longtime advocate with the National Union of the Homeless (NUH), called for a new campaign to finish King's unfinished business. Alongside leaders like Rev. Dr. William J. Barber II (Repairers of the Breach) and Rev. Dr. Liz Theoharis (Kairos Center), she launched the Poor People's Campaign: A National Call for Moral Revival. This campaign aimed to address deepening poverty, systemic racism, ecological devastation, militarism and the war economy, and the distorted moral narrative of religious nationalism. These leaders recognized that, as a nation, we were at a critical juncture. We needed a movement that would shift the moral narrative, influence policies and elections at every level of government, and build lasting power for poor and impacted people.

Dr. Martin, drawing from her experience with the National Union of the Homeless, emphasized the need for homeless and poor people to be at the forefront of this organizing work. The NUH was a national organization of and led by homeless people, active in the 1980s and '90s, reaching twenty-five chapters and around twenty-five thousand members at its height. It drew inspiration from the 1968 Poor People's Campaign and brought together poor and homeless people who were committed to ending poverty and human suffering for all. As the president of the Boston chapter in the 1980s, Dr. Martin explained that the Union was founded by former and current homeless individuals who were "organizing to take back what was ours: taking back our jobs; we were going to take back our children; we were going to take back our communities; we were going to take back the housing. . . . Homeless men and women in this country are displaced workers undergoing traumatic experiences from the conditions of poverty. And they needed to organize to bring about change."

In preparation for the 2018 campaign, Dr. Martin participated in mass meetings and trainings, including a significant event at Boston's Trinity Church where she delivered a powerful poem calling for justice and solidarity. As a lifelong organizer, she took the responsibility of calling for and organizing a new poor people's campaign seriously.

> It's my responsibility and accountability to do something, to make a contribution, just like those that came before me whose shoulders I stand on, who made a contribution to the movement to get us to this point. So as a woman in this struggle, a woman of color in this struggle, a woman who has felt the suffering across this nation, it's my responsibility to link arms in this sisterhood and in this brotherhood. It's an urgent time that we live in, it's an urgent time. People are dying, people need jobs, a livable wage, and it's gonna take each and every one of us to come on board and understand [and] educate. Each one teach one.

Savina Martin recognized the power of celebrating traditions of justice that have organized poor and dispossessed people throughout history. Her poem became a prayer for the movement, reminding all that God has called for a revolution of values. Echoing Mary's jubilant cries in the Magnificat, Savina declared that the powerful would be brought down and the poor lifted up, calling the community to unite in the fight against poverty and to create a society where justice and equity prevail.

PRAYER FOR A MOVEMENT ANNIVERSARY: THE LITANY

This litany is an adaptation of Dr. Savina Martin's poem "Ending Poverty." Visit the website to see Dr. Martin's reading of the original poem. 🌐

Reader 1: Poverty has got to go!
All: Poverty has got to go!
Reader 1: We are gathering up the children of the Poor People's Campaign of old. We are in the last trimester. We have birthed a new and unsettling force. Raising a generation of leaders led by the poor and dispossessed of this nation . . . we are organizing. We are building a movement, not a moment, but a movement that will raise its fist and shout, "The time has come!"

We are a new and unsettling voice, birthing out a new generation, a new way of life, living, and liberty. Setting the captives free,

Free—from a lifelong sentence of servitude, of never enough,
Free—from never enough food,
Free—from never enough money to pay my bills,
Free—from never enough grants for school and never enough good care for health care.

It's time to transform the Jericho Road. We are marking time as we saddle up the mule train in this hour to gather up the children of King and Chavez, gather up the Jesus kids, the Kennedy kids, Tubman's kids, and shout: We are here! Open the gates of the cities, the gates of the nations and the courts to those sentenced to the hard labor of servitude—earning less than fifteen. Open the gates to moral resistance RIGHT NOW! Not tomorrow, NOW!

King asked:

Reader 2: Who owns the oil? Who owns the iron ore? Why is it that poor people have to pay water bills in a world that is two-thirds water?

Reader 1: Gather the souls of this nation, from the Poor People's Campaign of old. Some folk thought it was aborted and permanently replaced by the four evils of racism, poverty, war and ecological devastation . . .

But ahhhh, it has been REVIVED at this hour.

We are here to raise our fist and say—NO more! No more do you have another day to regard us as human industrial waste. No more will you dump us onto the streets from our homes in order for your developers to build high-priced condominiums. No more! No more will I work for low wages. No more will my children go hungry after I pay my bills because my wages were not enough—no more. No more will I stand in a long soup line for stale bread. No more.

Poverty is trauma. PTSD. Poverty Trauma from a System Devalued. Living on the streets is trauma. Pushing a shopping cart to redeem the sticky cans from the trash bin lottery is trauma.

Reader 2: We are pregnant with a new and unsettling force of revolutionary values, and we are crystal clear—and hear the clarion call. We see the failure of a system, which is expressing itself in the form of systemic ills (poverty, war, homelessness, incarceration), a failure, this system has failed. Systemic oppression, mass incarceration, military war complexes that send our sons and daughters home in body bags. We shout NO more!

All: NO more!

Reader 1: Open the gates to the cities and climb the mountaintops of the villages ravaged by poverty, freeing ourselves from the shackles of despair. This system no longer provides the basic necessities for its people. We are fed up!

We are the offspring of the Poor People's Campaign, building a movement led by the poor—a new and unsettling voice! We must organize! The call:

Reader 2: We call your name, Black, white, Indigenous, Asian, Pacific Islander, LBGTQIA2S+, veterans, man, woman, religion, non-religion, God's people, all people, it is our human right . . .

We are calling you, COME OUT from the pews and the doorways of shame and onto the moral ground of resistance. We call on you to go block by block and organize the cadre of leaders, we call on you to educate the cadre, the revolutionaries to the National Call for Moral Revival . . . and with the report from the witnesses, change is gonna come.

Gather up the children, from Selma to Philadelphia, Mississippi to Albuquerque to Los Angeles to Charlottesville to Appalachia to the four corners of New England and the plazas of the Vatican, and on to the halls of Congress. Shout!

Reader 1: Saddle up the mule train—we have a movement to build, led by the poor and dispossessed. The time is now, take off the load. We are transforming the Jericho Road. Together, one voice, one fist, collectively we ignite the fire of resistance and shout: Poverty has got to go!

All: Poverty has got to go!

REFLECT, EMBODY, DISCUSS

1. Where have you seen or found the leadership of poor and dispossessed people in your life?
2. How have you taken time to affirm, cultivate, and celebrate the leadership of poor and dispossessed people?
3. Dr. Martin Luther King Jr. said, "There are millions of poor people in this country who have very little, or even nothing, to lose. If they can be helped to take action together, they will do so with a freedom and a power that will be a new and unsettling force in our complacent national life." What can we learn from recognizing that the systems that exploit us and deny us the ability to fully thrive are not worth saving? What freedom comes when we realize we have nothing to lose?

CHANT OF THE ANCESTORS: THE STORY

In July 2013, a group of one hundred young Black radical leaders from around the country gathered in Chicago for the Beyond November Movement Convening. While they were together, the George Zimmerman verdict in the killing of Trayvon Martin was delivered. As Black youth heard the words "not guilty," they collectively understood that American society didn't value Black life. This realization catalyzed the formation of Black Youth Project 100 (BYP100) as collective grief became a powerful force for change.

BYP100 became a member-based organization of Black eighteen-to-thirty-five-year-old activists and organizers dedicated to creating justice and freedom for all Black people. The membership core grounded their organizing model in the principles of decision-making and radical inclusivity, and is building a Black politics through a Black, queer, feminist lens.

From its inception, the organization understood the need to celebrate the beauty, the value, and the power of Black people while creating space to collectively mourn and hold each other's pain. This need led to a core value that stressed the importance of *holistic energy*: merging political education, artistic expression, and musical healing. This interdisciplinary approach aims to raise awareness, promote personal healing, surmount institutional barriers, and generate Black joy, love, self-care, and healing.

In a society that devalues Black and Brown humanity through the perpetuation of white supremacy, celebrating Black joy is not a luxury; it is a necessity for liberation. BYP100's *Black Joy Experience Resource Guide* emphasizes that "joy is not a means to an end, but the experience of joy and love is the end, it is the point, it is the reason we come together. To be able to joyfully live out our self-determined lives without limitations or barriers is why we exist."

The Black Joy Experience, a project spearheaded by Jonathan Lykes, a founding member of BYP100, exemplifies BYP100's emphasis on joy, healing, and holistic energy. This musical compilation of original Black freedom songs and liberation chants celebrates Black activism and political participation. Centering the principle of holistic energy to sustain the movement, BYP100's *Black Joy Experience Resource Guide* teaches freedom songs and liberation chants as a healing tool for centering, connecting, and communicating among young Black organizers. "Black joy comes alive and stays alive through our music," notes former BYP100 director Charlene Carruthers. "There is no way to think about the Black radical tradition without including how our ancestors, and we today, carry our resistance through sound . . . When I feel that all else is lost, sounds from our people lift me up."

BYP100 youth also turned to their ancestors to draw on a powerful legacy of freedom fighters who came before them. Central to BYP100's ethos is the "Ancestors Watching" chant, a powerful ritual rooted in the cultural, political, and spiritual heritage of New Orleans. Introduced by the artist CFreedom and Mike Molina in December 2015, the ritual originally involved turning off the lights and lighting candles to honor ancestors who were freedom fighters. Their names were spoken aloud before the flames were extinguished, symbolizing their enduring presence and guidance. Initially focusing on figures like Harriet Tubman and Ella Baker, the practice evolved to include participants' personal ancestors.

Jonathan Lykes played a crucial role in evolving the "Ancestors Watching" chant to further reflect the organization's core values. In 2016, the "Ancestors Watching" chant was remixed to weave together three crucial concepts: the presence of ancestors in the ongoing struggle for liberation, the significance of the Say Her Name campaign (highlighting the institutional violence faced by Black women and femmes like Sandra Bland), and the celebration of Black magic and beauty that is critical for the survival of Black people.

In 2016, Jonathan Lykes created a polyrhythmic exercise weaving these three concepts together. He did this believing that if we can encourage folks to sing, it not only shifts the energy in the room; it also allows for deeper moments of vulnerability and truth in movement work. Getting a generation of people to sing together becomes a metaphor for the power being built in the world.

Rituals and music have long been vital in the Black radical tradition, serving as tools of resistance and resilience. BYP100's practices, such as the "Ancestors Watching" chant and *The Black Joy Experience*, offer powerful examples of moral resistance and how the use of holistic energy can sustain our movements. These rituals offer a way to honor the past, energize the present, and foster deep connections within communities. BYP100's methods continue to inspire contemporary struggles for liberation and justice, demonstrating that honoring tradition and embracing holistic energy are essential for creating lasting change.

CHANT OF THE ANCESTORS: THE RITUAL

This song/chant, shared by Jonathan Lykes, was taught to BYP100 members at the Atlanta National Coordinating Council Convening in December of 2015, where CFreedom, the inaugural co-chair of the New Orleans chapter, gave BYP100 the chant/song. Say Her Name was a trans- and femme-led national Movement for Black Lives campaign response to the Sandra Bland police murder that took place on July 13, 2015. This became an outcry chant to lift up the names and voices of Black femmes impacted by systemic violence. "Black girl magic" was a term popularized by Cashawn Thompson in 2013. She created the term to represent the joy, beauty, power, and resilience of Black people living on the margins. This chant declares the importance of Black magic, led by Black women, to be conjured up by movement organizers, tapping into a radical imagination, and created through faith, love, and joy. 🌐

I know they're watching,
Ancestors watching,
I know they're watching, I know, I know

Say her name, Say her name,
Say her name, Say her name

Black Magic, Black Magic Raining Down,
Black Magic, Black Magic

REFLECT, EMBODY, DISCUSS

1. How do rituals like the "Ancestors Watching" chant contribute to the sense of community and purpose within BYP100? In what ways do these rituals honor the legacy of past freedom fighters while addressing contemporary struggles?
2. Why is the celebration of Black joy and the practice of holistic energy crucial to BYP100's mission? What practices help sustain you in your commitment to social justice today?
3. What can you learn from BYP100's emphasis on holistic energy and the integration of art, music, and healing in activism? What steps can you take to create spaces for joy, healing, and inclusivity in your work for justice?

SONG OF BELONGING FOR COMMUNITY ORGANIZING: THE STORY

This story was adapted from Anu Yadav's essay "Being Together: The Revolutionary Love of a Poor People's Movement" in We Are Civic Media. 🌐

In times of crisis, the powers of community and creativity can be lifelines, guiding us through difficult times. Anu's journey to find her place in a community of poor and dispossessed people building a movement to end poverty is a testament to this profound truth.

Anu's story began in 2002 when she moved to Washington, DC, and met Miss Debra, a charismatic leader fighting against the displacement of her community at the Arthur Capper/Carrollsburg public housing project, known as Cappers. Redevelopment efforts funded by the HOPE VI federal grant program threatened to displace four hundred Black families, despite promises of one-to-one replacement of low-income units.

Residents knew developers just wanted them gone, but they believed that by organizing, they could push for their needs to be prioritized. Where developers saw a "blighted" community, residents saw a community rich in love, pride, and mutual support.

Initially, Anu, a youth-theater educator, saw herself as an ally, detached from the struggles of poverty. She knocked on doors, helped with petitions, attended meetings, participated in community gardening and cleanups, and eventually taught youth-theater workshops. These experiences led her to interview residents and, with their permission, write a play based on their experiences, amplifying their voices and drawing attention to issues of gentrification and poverty.

Despite some victories, many original residents couldn't return to the redeveloped Cappers, and those who did faced new challenges as gentrification loomed. This highlighted the need for local efforts to connect with larger movements to achieve structural change.

Even as Anu organized alongside leaders like Miss Debra, Miss Rose, and Miss Agnes, she hadn't fully confronted her own economic struggles. Reflecting on her childhood, she realized that her family, though they always had food, struggled financially. After her father died, her mother juggled night shifts at Burger King and classes at a community college while raising Anu and her brother. They never named their situation as poverty, and the stigma silenced them, cutting off connections with others in similar situations.

Now, as a young adult in DC, Anu suddenly faced her own illegal eviction. Even as she worked to prevent the displacement of the others, she found herself in a precarious housing situation.

And guess who showed up for her? The Cappers community, led by mothers like Miss Debra and Miss Agnes. Their acts of kindness were expressions of solidarity and collective survival, helping Anu realize that the movement to end poverty was not just altruistic but a personal necessity.

In 2017, Anu shared her story of crisis at a mass meeting of the Poor People's Campaign in Los Angeles, realizing the power of collective storytelling. This moment transformed her understanding of her economic reality and connected her to the 140 million poor and low-wealth people in the United States who could not afford a four-hundred-dollar emergency—and millions more just a paycheck away.

By sharing her story, Anu found strength in numbers and discarded the shame associated with poverty. This was a moment of celebration, in which she knew deeply that she was part of the 140 million poor. She learned that this movement to end poverty had always been her movement too.

Luis Rodriguez, an author and poet, once told Anu, "When we're caught up in a crisis, creativity is a path out of it." This resonated deeply with her. Creativity, fueled by love and community, is vital for survival. Creative expression mirrors the resourcefulness required by anyone trying to survive in a society where poverty is a leading cause of death.

In 2023, Anu participated in collective study with artists and cultural organizers across the country, coordinated by the Kairos Center, focusing on cultivating revolutionary love in the movement. Reflecting on Dr. King's understanding of *agape* love—God's deep and unconditional love of humanity and a "willingness to go to any length to restore community"—Anu was reminded of the Hindu term *bhakti*, which refers to pure devotion and the understanding that God dwells within us all. As she studied this idea of revolutionary love in community with other artists and cultural organizers connected to struggles of the poor and dispossessed, Anu was inspired to celebrate this vision of revolutionary love and wrote a song called "We Belong Together."

The song expressed the need for society to embody *agape* and *bhakti*: a creative, redemptive, unconditional, and unsentimental kind of love. This love, practiced daily through organizing, collective struggle, and creative collaboration, is essential for reorganizing society from the bottom up, ensuring abundance and dignity for all.

Being part of this movement, understanding our own poverty, and connecting across differences allows us to more deeply understand and feel glimpses of this love. As we build true solidarity, we understand more clearly how we've been systematically isolated from each other. Coming together to build a movement is a practice in revolutionary love. Anu's story and her song remind us that by connecting across differences and celebrating revolutionary love, we can build an unstoppable force to create a brighter future for all.

WE BELONG TOGETHER: THE SONG

Anu Yadav, Los Angeles, wrote this song during the We Cry Justice Revolutionary Love Study and Creative Creation Series hosted by the Kairos Center. She shared it with the collective, inviting collaboration. Isaiah Briggs from Boston added the bridge, and other leaders contributed vocal harmonies. 🌐

Love is an action
A place to sleep
Love is to rise up
Standing with me

Love is together
Righting the wrong
Knowing there's a place
You always belong

We belong we belong we belong
We belong we belong together

Out of the mud
The lotus blooms
Hearts wide open
With the truth

Seeking justice
Seeking peace
Linking arms
We're gonna get free

We belong we belong we belong
We belong we belong together

Break the lie of loneliness
Break it with love
There's a place for you
There's a place for us

A place for you
Here in my heart
Come right home
To the truth of my arms

To the truth of my arms

We belong we belong we belong
We belong we belong together

We are not broken
We are not too much
We are powerful
We are enough

We are enough

We belong we belong we belong
We belong we belong together

(*Bridge*)
Together we can, together we will
Together we stand, together we build
A whole new world, it's time to get real
There's something inside I know we all feel
The power of love they try to conceal
So don't hide it in a bush; time to put it on a hill
Cause hand in hand's the way that we heal
And hand in hand I know that we will
Cause they can never tear us apart
When we're living from the love that is in our heart
Say they can never tear us apart
When we're living from the love that is in our heart
So fill our hearts with holy fire
Unite us with our sole desire
Cause we are of our family
Time together in unity

Cause we belong we belong we belong
We belong we belong together

REFLECT, EMBODY, DISCUSS

1. How does the concept of "revolutionary love," as discussed by Anu and other artists, relate to the struggle against poverty and injustice? How do the terms *agape* and *bhakti* enhance the understanding of this love in the context of community organizing?
2. How did Anu's act of vulnerability encourage others to recognize and speak about their own struggles, and connect people to the movement to end poverty? Reflect on how those close you or those

around you might be experiencing poverty. Consider how job loss, medical emergencies, or unexpected expenses could affect your financial stability.

3. What themes are expressed in the song "We Belong Together," and how do they reflect the broader message of Anu's story? How does the collaborative nature of the song's creation reinforce the message of community and solidarity?

CHAPTER SIX

LITURGIES OF THE PEOPLE

WE EMBARK NOW on a final journey through the realms of prayer, poetry, and song that are shaped by the struggles and triumphs of poor and dispossessed communities. While the resources in the previous chapters were specifically designed for rituals of remembrance, celebration, lamentation, healing, and action, the liturgies in this chapter can be used in a variety of ways and for various purposes.

Liturgy derives from a Greek word that means "the work of the people." The liturgies in this final chapter serve as a testament to the enduring spirit of resilience, resistance, and revolution that is the lifeblood of the Freedom Church of the Poor tradition. At the heart of these liturgies is a shared commitment to dismantling systems of oppression and inequality. As we wrote in the introduction, you are free to use and adapt these liturgies to fit your own context. As you read these concluding pages, consider what aspects of these liturgies speak to your community. How might you honor the communities that gave birth to these liturgies while still making them relevant for the community in which you live?

Whether these liturgies are shared in public gatherings or read in moments of private reflection, we hope they offer solace, strength, and vision to all who are engaged in the daily struggle for dignity and justice. Through these liturgies, we raise our voices in solidarity with the poor and dispossessed. Through these rituals, we discover renewed strength and conviction to fight for a world in which everyone is valued, everyone is heard, and everyone, finally, is free.

LITANY FOR A KAIROS MOVEMENT

An Interfaith Litany for Building Power

This litany was shared at the 2013 launch of the Kairos Center for Religion, Rights, and Social Justice at Union Theological Seminary. The event brought together scholars, religious leaders, artists, and activists for a conference titled Rights and Religions: A Movement Breaking Through. The day concluded with an evening of hope, highlighting voices calling for a new reality. The litany was written by Rev. Dr. Derrick McQueen, pastor of St. James Presbyterian Church and associate director of the Center on African American Religion, Sexual Politics, and Social Justice at Columbia University.

Reader 1: Mahatma Gandhi: "Power based on love is a thousand times more effective and permanent then the one derived from fear of punishment."

All: Gandhi teaches that love and hope bring more good than hatred and vengeance.

Reader 2: Vandana Shiva: "Earth rights are also the rights of humans as they flow from the rights of Mother Earth: the right to food and water, the right to health and a safe environment, and the right to the commons—the rivers, the seas, land, and forests."

All: Vandana Shiva teaches us that all life's justice springs from the wisdom of Mother Earth.

Reader 3: Joe Hill: "Goodbye Bill. I die like a true blue rebel. Don't waste any time in mourning. Organize. . . ."

All: Joe Hill teaches us to continue fighting for those we love and miss.

Reader 4: Badshah Khan, nonviolent soldier of Islam: "If you want your country and your people to prosper you must stop living for yourselves alone. You must start living for the community."

All: Badshah Khan teaches us the only way to prosperity and progress.

Reader 5: Rabbi Abraham Joshua Heschel: "When faith is completely replaced by creed, worship by discipline, love by habit; when the crisis of today is ignored because of the splendor of the past; when faith becomes an heirloom rather than a living fountain; when religion speaks only in the name of authority rather than with the voice of compassion—its message becomes meaningless."

All: Abraham Joshua Heschel teaches us that religion is at its best when it's held to its foundational beliefs.

Reader 6: Harriet Tubman: "Don't ever stop. Keep going. If you want a taste of freedom, keep going."

All: Harriet Tubman teaches us why we keep going.

Reader 7: Martin Luther King Jr.: "Human progress is neither automatic nor inevitable . . . Every step toward the goal of justice requires sacrifice, suffering, and struggle; the tireless exertions and passionate concern of dedicated individuals."

All: Martin Luther King Jr. teaches us to give all we are for all that is right.

All: Oscar Romero teaches and reminds us, "When we struggle for human rights, for freedom, for dignity, when we feel that it is a ministry of the church to concern itself for those who are hungry, for those who have no schools, for those who are deprived, we are not departing from God's promise. The church knows it is saving the world when it undertakes to speak also of such things."

COMMUNION LITURGY

A Bilingual Liturgy for the Freedom Church of the Poor

Variations of this liturgy are used in regular Communion services with the Freedom Church of the Poor and La Iglesia del Pueblo. Adapted by Dr. Adam Barnes and Arelis Figueroa, it draws on a variety of Communion liturgies, including: Katherine Hawker's Communion Liturgy, Cláudio Carvalhaes's Liturgies from Below: Praying with People at the End of the World, *Joe Paparone's FCOP Communion Liturgy, Liz Theoharis's Communion Liturgy, and the Presbyterian Communion Liturgy. The liturgy below was used during Pride Month services with FCOP and La Iglesia del Pueblo.*

Spanish: Así como en las primeras comunidades cristianas, cuándo estamos organizándonos con la intención de satisfacer las necesidades de los pobres quienes son marginados de la abundancia; y para defender los proyectos revolucionarios de los pueblos organizados hoy día, llegamos a esta mesa porque compartimos la visión de un mundo liberado. Venimos de luchas y experiencias diferentes a esta mesa, donde todas y todos somos bienvenidos y reconocidos en nuestra diversidad.

English: Like in the first Christian communities, as we both strive to organize to meet the needs of the poor who are outcast in the land of plenty and as we defend the revolutionary projects of the organized poor today, we come to this table because we share a vision of a liberated world. We come from our different struggles and experiences to this table where we are all welcome and seen in our diversity.

English: Today, like then, we struggle under an oppressive system. We are considered to be inferior based on our race, ethnicity, sexual orientation, gender identity, or geographical location. Where the religion of empire may turn us away from this table, we celebrate a true faith in God's infinite love. Therefore, at this table we are welcomed fully for who we are and seen as we want to be.

Spanish: Similar a nuestras realidades, estas comunidades vivian bajo un sistema opresor en donde eran considerados inferiores debido a su raza, etnia, orientación sexual, identidad de género, o posición geográfica. Aún cuando la religión del imperio quiere expulsarlos de esta mesa, hoy celebramos la fe verdadera, al Dios del amor infinito. Entonces, aquí en esta mesa, todas las personas son bienvenidas completa y exactamente como son.

Spanish: En esta mesa recordamos que Dios elige a los pobres y condena a los ricos una y otra vez. Recordamos las historias del pan compartido, multitudes alimentadas, historias de encuentros entre enemigos y amigos, rechazados y marginados, juntos alrededor de la mesa. Hoy también celebramos las familias y comunidades que hemos encontrado y construido junto a quienes también han sido rechazados injustamente. Aquí todos somos hijos e hijas de Dios.

English: At this the table of remembrance, we remember that God chooses the poor and condemns the rich over and over again. We remember the stories of bread broken and shared, feeding a multitude. Stories of being gathered, enemy and friend, outcast and marginalized, together around tables. Today we also celebrate a family and community that we may have found and built with others who have also been rejected unjustly. Here we are all God's children.

English: This evening, we remember a meal where Jesus was gathered with his disciples on the eve of his crucifixion, where he would be killed as a threat to the empire because he was committed to a revolutionary project. In spite of being in the midst of the doubts and betrayal of his followers, Jesus celebrated the community and the possibility of a reign of justice and peace with them.

Spanish: Esta noche, recordamos una comida donde Jesús estaba reunido con sus discípulos, la víspera de su crucifixión donde sería asesinado por ser una amenaza para el imperio por su proyecto revolucionario. A pesar de encontrarse en medio de la duda y la traición de sus seguidores, Jesús celebró con ellos la comunidad y la posibilidad de un reino de paz y justicia.

Spanish: Ahora, les invitamos a que juntos nos acerquemos a la mesa de Comunión, tenemos un pedazo de pan y jugo y bendigamos y compartamos juntos.

English: We now invite you to join us at the table for Communion. If you would like, we invite you to grab a piece of bread and juice that we may bless and share together.

Invitation to the Table/Invitación a la Mesa

English: At this table we all come from communities that know hunger and thirst. We come with a shared heart and spirit. Here we are invited to remember how Jesus ate and drank to forge relationships across boundaries. We come free of judgment, invited to leave our prejudices, shortcomings, and doubts aside, to receive this blessing.

Spanish: En esta mesa vinimos desde comunidades que han conocido el hambre y la sed. Vinimos con un corazón y espíritu compartido. En esta mesa estamos invitados a recordar cómo Jesús comió y bebió para forjar relaciones más allá de las fronteras. Venimos libres de juicio, invitados a dejar de lado nuestros prejuicios, carencias y dudas, para recibir esta bendición.

Dios santo, te pedimos que nos de tu bendicion en esta comida y bebida compartida. Transfórmanos ahora para que podamos vivir, movernos y respirar juntos como uno solo.

Ven, Espíritu Santo, vuélvenos a formar como criaturas de un mundo donde todos estamos dentro, nadie está afuera, para que podamos seguir la dirección del Espíritu hacia esa meta a la cual avanzamos . . . tu reino en la tierra donde todos tenemos derecho a vivir, en un sistema justo "con todos y para el bien de todos."

English: Gracious God, we ask you to rain blessings upon this shared meal and drink. Transform us now that we may live and move and breathe together as one. Come, Holy Spirit, re-form us as creatures of a world where everybody is in, nobody is out, that we may follow the Spirit's leading toward that goal to which we press on . . . your reign on earth where everybody has a right to live and we lift from the bottom so that everybody may rise.

And just as Jesus gathered with the people, he took the bread and said, "Take, eat, all of you. This is my body broken for you. Whenever you eat it, remember me and all those who have died striving for justice."

Spanish: Jesus, reunido con la gente, tomó el pan y dijo:

"Tomad, comed todos. Este es mi cuerpo partido por ti. Siempre que lo comas, acuérdense de mí y de todos los que han muerto luchando por la justicia."

English: In the same way, he took the cup after supper, blessed it and shared it, saying, "Take this cup and drink of it all of you. This cup is the cup of life, rebirth, justice. Whenever you drink, remember me and all those who have died from injustice."

We offer this bread and cup to all, to you—the eager, the doubtful, the ones who know a new community and world is possible. We strive for a global society built around solidarity and peace instead of war and violence.

So come, all you who hunger and thirst for food and justice. Come and be filled.

Spanish: De la misma manera, tomó la copa después de la cena, la bendijo y la compartió, diciendo: "Tomen esta copa y beban todos de ella. Esta copa es la copa de la vida, del renacimiento, de la justicia. Siempre que bebas, acuérdate de mí y de todos los que han muerto por la injusticia."

Ofrecemos este pan y esta copa a todos, a ustedes, a los ansiosos, a los que dudan, a los que saben que una nueva comunidad y mundo es posible. Queremos una sociedad global construida en base a la solidaridad y la paz, en vez de la guerra y violencia.

Vengan todos los que tienen hambre y sed de alimento y de justicia. Vengan y reciban.

English: A place has been prepared for you.

Spanish: Se ha preparado un lugar para ti.

English: The gifts of God for the people of God.

Spanish: Los dones de Dios para el pueblo de Dios.

COVID-19 MEMORIAL

An Interfaith Litany for Healing and Justice

In June 2022, the Poor People's Campaign brought tens of thousands of poor and low-wealth people to Washington, DC, for a Mass Poor People's and Low-Wage Worker's Assembly and Moral March to share their stories and address systemic injustices worsened by the pandemic. This interfaith litany was part of the Everybody's Got a Right to Live Memorial Service, held in Washington, DC, on June 17, 2022. It was written by the Rev. Dr. Jessica Williams of the Kairos Center and the Kansas Poor People's Campaign. 🌐

Reader 1: We stand together as witnesses of the loss, the grief, and the suffering caused by the death-dealing systems in our nation and the lives that have been taken due to COVID-19, poverty, systemic racism, militarism and war, ecological devastation, and the distorted moral narrative of Christian nationalism.

Reader 2: We join together with the ancient witnesses of our faiths, drawing from our sacred texts for guidance and strength to weep, wail, and mourn until we finally get the nation's attention and together repent and change.

Reader 3: Like the prophet Muhammad when his child died, and he wept and said, "Verily the eyes shed tears and the heart grieves," we shed tears and our hearts grieve for the over one million lives taken by COVID-19 in the United States and over six million worldwide (Ṣaḥīḥ al-Bukhārī 1241).

All Voices: We weep. We wail. We mourn. Until we call attention. We repent. We change.

Reader 4: Like Rachel, we weep and we wail for our children. For the twenty-one children and adults who died from gun violence in Texas, and all those families who weep and wail because their children are no more. With Rachel, we refuse to be consoled because our children are no more (Jeremiah 31:15; Matthew 2:18).

All Voices: We weep. We wail. We mourn. Until we call attention. We repent. We change.

Reader 2: Like Jesus who looked upon the city of Jerusalem and wept, we too look upon the cities, towns, and countryside of this nation and weep for land being destroyed by fracking, coal ash ponds, pollution, and deforestation (Luke 19:41).

All Voices: We weep. We wail. We mourn. Until we call attention. We repent. We change.

Reader 4: Like Mordecai who, when he learned of the orders to kill his people, put on sackcloth and ashes and went into the city and wailed loudly and bitterly, we too wail in sackcloth and ashes for our people killed by police brutality, for lives lost to war, and for all affected by militarism and the war economy (Esther 4:1).

All Voices: We weep. We wail. We mourn. Until we call attention. We repent. We change.

Reader 2: Like the Psalmist who cried out to God for help on the day of distress, we too call out on behalf of the seven hundred people who die every day from poverty in the richest country in the world (Psalm 102:1–2).

All Voices: We weep. We wail. We mourn. Until we call attention. We repent. We change.

Reader 1: With our Indigenous relatives and our Buddhist siblings we recognize that we are all interconnected and the suffering of one is the suffering of all.

All Voices: We weep. We wail. We mourn. Until we call attention. We repent. We change.

Reader 3: And with our Hindu siblings we pray:

All Voices: May all be happy.
May all be free from disease.
May all know that which is good.
May none suffer.
Amen. (Traditional Hindu prayer.)

CREDO DE INMIGRANTE

A Bilingual Immigrant Creed

This Immigrant Creed was developed by leaders of Iglesia del Pueblo in New York City. It draws on the following creeds for inspiration: "Hispanic Creed," by Rev. Dr. Justo Gonzalez; "The Immigrant Creed," by Rev. Jose Luis Casal; and "Credo del Pueblo Inmigrante," by Un Pueblo en Marcha.

Credo de Inmigrante

Creemos en Dios Padre y Madre creadora de los cielos y de la tierra, creadora de pueblos y culturas, de los idiomas y las razas.

Creemos en Dios que defiende el derecho de las mujeres, de los niños y las niñas, de los jornaleros en las esquinas, de los pobres y de los inmigrantes. Un Dios que derriba las fronteras, las diferencias y los grandes poderes.

El Dios que guió a su pueblo en el exilio y en el éxodo, el Dios de José en Egipto, de Daniel en Babilonia, de Hagar en el desierto,el Dios de los extranjeros e inmigrantes, quien está a nuestro lado mientras cruzamos desiertos, mares, y ríos, como el río bravo y selvas como la del Darién, el Dios que nos protege en medio de la oscuridad y al dormir en las calles de pueblos desconocidos.

El Dios de los profetas, reformadores, mártires de la fe y santos anónimos de ayer y hoy, el Dios en quien creyeron y confiaron Agustin, Teresa de Avila, Martin Luthero, el mismo que inspiró a Bertha Caceres, Minerva Mirabal, Cecilia Mujica, Mariana de Jesus, Harriet Tubman, Cesar Chavez, y a Oscar Arnulfo Romero.

Creemos en Jesucristo—su hijo—un desplazado Judeo-Palestino, quien nació lejos de su gente y de su casa, quien, como muchos de nosotros, huyó de su pais con sus padres cuando su vida estuvo en peligro, y al volver tuvo que sufrir la opresión del tirano Poncio Pilato, el sirviente de un potencia extranjera. Fue perseguido, golpeado, torturado y finalmente acusado y condenado a muerte injustamente. Pero, en el tercer día, este Jesús rechazado resucitó de la muerte, no como un extranjero sino para ofrecernos la ciudadanía de su reino dándonos esperanza de vida nueva.

Creemos en el Espíritu Santo, el inmigrante eterno del Reino de Dios entre nosotros/as/es, que habla todos los idiomas, vive en todos los países y une a todas la razas. Quien nos sostiene cada día, quien nos da fuerzas para no rendirnos y levantarnos cuando caemos.

Creemos en la Iglesia como un hogar seguro para todos los extranjeros e inmigrantes, donde hemos encontrado apoyo, refugio y solaz. Una Iglesia donde todos hablan el mismo idioma: el del amor y tienen el mismo propósito: la paz y la justicia.

Creemos que la comunión de los santos comienza cuando aceptamos la diversidad de los santos. Creemos en el perdón, el cual nos hace iguales y en la reconciliación, que nos identifica mucho más que una raza, lengua o nacionalidad.

Creemos en la resurrección, como el día de la gran fiesta, donde estaremos unidos como pueblo, celebrando nuestra unidad en la diversidad.

Creemos en la vida eterna más allá de este mundo, donde nadie será inmigrante sino que todos seremos ciudadanos/as/es del Reino de Dios que no tendrá fin.

Amén.

The Immigrant Creed

We believe in God the Father and Mother, Creator of the heavens and the earth, Creator of peoples and cultures, languages and races.

We believe in God who defends the rights of women and children, of day laborers on street corners, of the poor, and of immigrants. A God who breaks down borders, differences and great powers.

The God who guided his people in exile and in the exodus, the God of Joseph in Egypt, of Daniel in Babylon, of Hagar in the desert, the God of foreigners and immigrants, who is at our side while we cross deserts, seas, and rivers like the Rio Bravo, and jungles like the Darien, the God who protects us in the midst of darkness and when we sleep in the streets of unknown towns.

The God of the prophets, reformers, martyrs of the faith and anonymous saints of yesterday and today, the God in whom

Augustine, Teresa of Ávila, and Martin Luther believed and trusted, the same one who inspired Berta Cáceres, Minerva Mirabal, Cecilia Mujica, Mariana de Jesús de Paredes, Harriet Tubman, Cesar Chavez, and Oscar Arnulfo Romero.

We believe in Jesus Christ—his son—a displaced Palestinian-Jew born far from his people and his home who, like many of us, fled his country with his parents when his life was in danger, and upon his return had to suffer the oppression of the tyrant Pontius Pilate, the servant of a foreign power. He was persecuted, beaten, tortured, and finally unjustly accused and condemned to death. But, on the third day, this rejected Jesus rose from the dead, not as a foreigner but to offer us citizenship in his kingdom, giving us hope for new life.

We believe in the Holy Spirit, the eternal immigrant of the Kingdom of God among us, who speaks all languages, lives in all countries, and unites all races. Who sustains us every day, who gives us strength not to give up and to get up when we fall.

We believe in the church as a safe home for all foreigners and immigrants, where we have found support, refuge, and solace. A church where everyone speaks the same language, that of love, and has the same purpose: peace and justice.

We believe that the communion of saints begins when we accept the diversity of the saints. We believe in forgiveness, which makes us equal, and in reconciliation, which identifies us much more than a race, language, or nationality.

We believe in the resurrection, as the day of the great *fiesta*, where we will be united as a people, celebrating our unity in diversity. We believe in eternal life beyond this world, where no one will be an immigrant, but we will all be citizens of the Kingdom of God that will have no end.

Amen.

THE DISABLED: A PRAYER FOR THE ORDINARY

A Prayer for Justice and Inclusion

This prayer was written by the Rev. Chris Wylie, a United Methodist ordained elder, disability activist, and justice seeker who is active in many spaces, including with the Kairos Center and the Poor People's Campaign in New York state.

Today, we call upon a new spirit!
A spirit of justice and inclusion
We call for a world where we are no longer looked upon as special merely for our existence
A place where our needs are ordinary
A place where it is no longer necessary to be set apart as superheroes
Known to society simply as friends, as partners, as people, part of our collective oneness
In this place where togetherness reigns in the recognition of our shared unity as well as in our individual identity
May we claim and create this space where our rights exist fully and completely
No matter the bodies in which we live
Where we walk, roll, stand, or stroll just as we come
May we make it so, until it is so, without exception.

EARTH LITURGY

A Liturgy of Resistance to Climate Chaos

Rev. Chelsea MacMillan and Rev. Micah Bucey wrote this liturgy for a GreenFaith protest at JPMorganChase headquarters on Madison Avenue, opposing the bank's immoral funding of climate chaos. This nonviolent ritual, part of Climate Week NYC and preceding the March to End Fossil Fuels, used the People's mic call-and-response method as protesters chanted in a somber yet fiery ritual of lament for the earth. They demanded Chase stop funding new oil and gas projects and invest in renewable energy and communities most impacted by climate change. Between litanies honoring ecological disasters, protesters sang: "When the fires burn / And the seas rise / Not in our name / We say not in our name." 🌐

Opening Invocation

Reader 1:

We gather today in fear and in hope,
We gather in awe and in lament for the wonders of our natural world.
We gather in anger here in the belly of the beast,
Just one branch of the insidious tendrils of greed proliferated by JP Morgan Chase Bank.

Reader 2:

As the burning of fossil fuels destroys our planet,
We refuse to allow the fires to destroy our belief that there is another way.
As we gather on the ancestral land of the Lenape people,
We honor the power of indigenous care for our planet,
And we commit to embodying this communal care ourselves.

Reader 3:

We bring our various faiths and our unified despair,
We bring our distinct sacred traditions and our collective rage,
We are united in incensed anger, but our demands are incredibly clear:
JP Morgan Chase Bank:
As one of the first fossil fuel investors and as a continuing agent of climate chaos,
We demand that you put an immediate end to new fossil fuel projects and deforestation.

We demand that you ensure a rapid transition to 100 percent renewable energy practices and a fair phase-out of fossil fuels.
We demand that you commit to a just transition for impacted workers and climate-vulnerable communities.

Reader 4:

These demands are the bare minimum requirements.
They are not requests. They are necessities.
We are burning with fury, but we refuse to burn out.
Instead, we gather here to allow the four elements of our planet to be our guide.
Each of these elements, earth, air, fire, and water, contain wisdom, but they all also contain warnings when they are out of balance.

Reader 5:

With earth as our inspiration, we ground ourselves.
With air as our inspiration, we honor the breath of life.
With fire as our inspiration, we brave the heat.
With water as our inspiration, we become the waves of change.

Reader 6:

You, JP Morgan Chase Bank, can also join us in grounding, breathing, braving, and becoming.
But you will have to give up the greed of green money and lean into the need for greener living.
Your fossil fuel burning, your money burning has been done not in our name.

Reader 7:

Only a cleansing of this space and every corner that you have affected
Will bring a new kind of change.
Today, we sanctify and cleanse this space and we urge you to feel the heat.

Song: Not in Our Name

When the fires burn
And the seas rise
Not in our name
We say not in our name

When the oil burns
And the stocks rise
Not in our name
We say not in our name

When the gas burns
And the planet dies
Not in our name
We say not in our name

When you choose greed
And tell us lies
Not in our name
We say not in our name

Movement I: Grounding Ourselves. Reader 1

[Following a three-minute reflection (written and read by a local faith leader), read these five remembrances with the refrain "Not in our name / We say not in our name" sung in call-and-response between each entry. A pile of earth is placed on the altar.]

Fracking
Mountaintop Removal
Desertification
Ruined crops
Endangered species

Movement II: Honoring the Breath of Life. Reader 2

[Following a three-minute reflection (written and read by a local faith leader), read these five remembrances with the refrain "Not in our name / We say not in our name" sung in call-and-response between each entry. Breath is breathed onto the pile of earth.]

Hurricane Katrina
Hurricane Sandy
Hurricane Maria
Tornadoes
Typhoons & Cyclones

Movement III: Braving the Heat. Reader 3

[Following a three-minute reflection (written and read by a local faith leader), read these five remembrances with the refrain "Not in our name / We say not in our name" sung in call-and-response between each entry. Dollar bills are burned and placed on the pile of earth.]

Canada wildfires
California wildfires
Maui
Greece
Australia

Movement IV: Becoming the Wave of Change. Reader 4

[Following a three-minute reflection (written and read by a local faith leader), read these five remembrances with the refrain "Not in our name / We say not in our name" sung in call-and-response between each entry. Water is poured onto the burned dollar bills.]

Floods in Pakistan
Bleached coral
Melting glaciers

Pacific Islands disappearing
Ocean acidification

Benediction

Reader 1:

Our actions today are symbolic, but they are not meaningless.
You, JP Morgan Chase Bank, can give them meaning with your own action.
Your name is synonymous with the destruction of creation.
You must turn around and unite your name with the re-creation of creation.

Reader 2:

JP Morgan Chase Bank:
As one of the first fossil fuel investors and as a continuing agent of climate chaos, we demand that you put an immediate end to new fossil fuel projects and deforestation. We demand that you ensure a rapid transition to 100 percent renewable energy practices and a fair phase-out of fossil fuels. We demand that you commit to a just transition for impacted workers and climate-vulnerable communities.

Reader 3:

Until these demands are met, we will return. We refuse to simply let our anger burn. With earth as our inspiration, we ground ourselves. With air as our inspiration, we honor the breath of life. With fire as our inspiration, we brave the heat. With water as our inspiration, we become the waves of change.
Cleanse your name.

[*As the action moves to the next level, "Not in Our Name" is repeated. Flowers are moved so that they cover the burned dollar bills to create an image of beautiful possibility where there was once destruction.*]

POEM FOR A HUNGER STRIKE

Words of Faith in a Time of War

Azmera Hammouri-Davis shared this poem as part of a week-long hunger strike calling for a permanent ceasefire in front of the White House. This week of action was called to illustrate the policy of starvation that Israel's attack on Gaza was enforcing. Hammouri-Davis (@azmerarhymes) is a writer, artist, and theologian from Kea'au, Hawaii, with family roots in Palestine. She is a founding organizer with Black Christians for Palestine, and currently based in Los Angeles (Tongva).

"Faith is being sure of what we hope for, and certain of what we do not yet see." Hebrews 11:11

Dear God,
My heart is breaking and I am feeling numb,
Wondering if the words will ever come
The sky is falling and the air is frail
How long must they live in this oppressive hell?

My mind is racing
Yet thoughts won't come out,
Why don't they seem to hear us when we shout?
Homes have been demolished, lives destroyed
What Good is left when all seems devoid.

As the narrative war rages on
The apartheid state drops bomb after bomb
And the U.S. govt claps as if they can do no wrong
What a sad, pitiful, shameful song.

But the people still gather
The masses still draw near
Together we lift our voices

Cast away every single doubt or fear
For the Lord sees every single cry and tear.

As the hurt, anger, and helplessness settle into our bones
We say we need not walk this journey alone.
So we pick up the phone, pick up the phone.
Not the U.S. president sanctioning another drone
With our tax dollars,
Pick up the phone
What would you do if this was your home?
And so we will continue to pick up the phone.

A RAMADAN RITUAL

A Fast from Evil and Oppression During Ramadan

This Ramadan reflection, later turned into a Ramadan prayer, was offered by Dr. Jamel Coy Hudson during the 2024 Lenten Worship series with The Kairos Center's Freedom Church of the Poor and partners. Dr. Hudson, a lecturer, professor, and rhetorician, is a former tri-chair of the New York state Poor People's Campaign: A National Call for Moral Revival, and a powerful theomusicologist in the movement. On the eve of Ramadan, he invited participants to the Freedom Mosque of the Poor, emphasizing the significance of Ramadan in today's world: "We are living in a time where the killing of innocent life and the suffering of humanity is something we can't turn our backs to. There is such pain and anguish in the land, and I, as a Muslim, while observing the fast and going through the rituals, must never forget the suffering of humanity."

This Ramadan, *insha'Allah*
May we make this month more than just a ritual
But may the forgoing of food for a month

remind us of those who are hungry every day
As we put ourselves in a little discomfort for a short period
May we remember those who are in pain and agony every single day.
May every meal we skip remind us never to forget
Starving children, children in poverty, in war, in shelters,
and under occupation.
May we remember mothers
cradling their children as they give their last breath.
As we thirst for water,
May we remember those who will never have water to quench their thirst.
If we forget,
If we get caught up in our rituals and don't hear the cry of the poor,
If we do not bear witness and act,
Then all our fasting is in vain.
The Prophet Muhammad (peace be upon him) said,
"Whoever does not give up forged speech and evil actions,
Allah is not in need of his leaving his food and drink
(i.e., Allah will not accept his fasting)."
This Ramadan, let us fast from evil and oppression.
O you who believe,
be upholders of justice.
Stand with those who are oppressed and resist zulm (injustice).
Resist injustice.
Speak the truth.
Let the fast you undertake remind you never to forget the least among us.
May Allah strengthen our hearts so that our fast is accepted.
May we continue to struggle for those living under occupation and violence.
May we come together as a community that sees the humanity in all of us,

and may we work to correct injustices and build a more just society
for all,
as we are all children of Adam.
Ameen.

I leave you with peace.
I wish you a blessed, justice-focused Ramadan.
Ramadan Mubarak!
As-salaam alaykum.

COMMISSIONING CELEBRATION

A Litany for Organizers

This litany was written for the First Annual Poverty Initiative Fellows Commissioning and Community Celebration, sponsored by the Poverty Initiative (now the Kairos Center) at Union Theological Seminary, a community committed to raising up religious and community leaders dedicated to building a social movement to end poverty, led by the poor. It can be adapted for the commissioning of a variety of workers, ministers, organizers, and others. 🌐

Reader 1: We gather today as a community. We gather as students, professors, alumni, trustees, administrators, friends, family. We gather as a people called and committed to respond to what Archbishop Oscar Romero declared the church's role: "To serve the people . . . to defend the cause of the poor and all that is human in the people's struggle." We gather to recognize where we have been on this journey for justice, where we now stand, and where we are going. This journey has changed us.

All: We can no longer judge things the way we used to.

Reader 2: We gather today, knowing that we are part of something much larger. We are surrounded by the cloud of witnesses who have shaped us and made us who we are. Those leaders that we have read and studied. Those who committed their intellect, passion, and their bodies to the struggle to proclaim God's radical love. Those who gave their lives over to something larger than themselves. Their witness has changed us.

All: We can no longer judge things the way we used to.

Reader 3: We gather today, conscious of the current crisis in which we find ourselves and are called to lead. It is in this political, social, and economic context that we are called to be authentic to the mission of Christ in our service and work for liberation. We are committed because our conscience gives us no other choice.

All: We can no longer judge things the way we used to.

Reader 4: We gather today to find strength for the journey. Martin Luther King Jr. reminds us that "Every step toward the goal of justice requires sacrifice, suffering, and struggle; the tireless exertions and passionate concern of dedicated individuals. . . . This is no time for apathy or complacency. This is the time for vigorous and positive action."

All: We can no longer judge things the way we used to.

Reader 5: But above all, we gather today to celebrate. We celebrate the Poverty Initiative Fellows, their commitments, talents, creativity, and gifts, offered in service to building a movement to end Poverty led by the poor. We gather to hold up their journeys in their work with the Poverty Initiative over the past year. We celebrate the victories, the lessons, and above all the people who make up this movement.

All: Let us celebrate and rejoice!

INVOCATION FOR THE FUTURE

A Prayer for Beautifully Varied People

This invocation by Ari Douglas was offered at an event of the Wisconsin Poor People's Campaign: A National Call for Moral Revival. Douglas is a leader in the Poor People's Campaign and the Freedom Church of the Poor. They have been involved in political movements with a focus on and fighting for the rights of low-income and LGBTQIA2S+ *people.*

Today, we gather in the spaces that we are creating sacred with the work that we are undertaking.
To stand for what is right and speak out against what is wrong.
To challenge those systems that have become, perhaps in their very creation, institutions that do not lift up but rather harm the poor and low-income individuals of Wisconsin.
To claim our right as people of conscience to stand for what is right and to frame the struggle that we are devoted to in this time and place.

I call on you at this time to look in one another's eyes, recognize the beautifully created humanity that is within each person here.
Though we are varied, it is through such moral fusion that we will win the fight for dignity and survival.
Today we renew our dedication to each other, that we might achieve the first steps of success in achieving what is needed for all people.
Given that Saturday is Transgender Remembrance Day we also remember the over thirty people who have been killed by hate based violence this year alone.

I invite you to join me in prayer or quiet meditation:

Great Spirit, you who are the parent to us all, you who have called us each by name and brought us to this place . . . you who blessed the Prophet Isaiah with the words to proclaim the Jubilee Year, The Spirit of the Lord is upon me because the Lord has anointed me to proclaim good news to the poor. They have sent me to bind up the brokenhearted, to proclaim liberty to the captives and release of the prisoners to proclaim the year of the Lord's favor.

I thank the divine who is known in so many different ways and by many different names for bringing us, a beautifully varied people, together.
I ask that we might be strengthened; that love and unity might conquer hatred and fear.
I ask that the rainbow of races might not live in fear of what the authorities may do to them,
I ask that LGBTQIA2S+ folx may be treated fairly and with love,
I ask that those who have uteruses may no longer be oppressed in this state or any other state, I ask that authorities might listen to our cries for justice which come from the deep lamentation of a hurt and bleeding people.
For someone is hurting our siblings, and it has gone on for far too long.
We pray that our grief and mourning may be replaced with joy and celebration.
That you use our hands and feet to rebuild our institutions that have been defiled by white supremacists.
We ask that you give us the strength to stand in righteousness and truth in this age, for you have written righteousness and hope upon our hearts.
We ask that all those who are here, whether they support us or not, may live in safety and security, and that peace may reign.
Most of all may that single word which is our state motto be made true.
Forward. Forward into a future where we have a government that works for us not against us. Forward into a future where all can vote.
Forward into a future where everyone can make a decent wage.
All this we pray to the one of many names.
Amen.

PRAYER FOR PENTECOST

A Prayer of Good News of the Spirit

This prayer for Pentecost was written by Tim Shenk, a bilingual movement educator. He is a leader with the University of the Poor and the New York State Poor People's Campaign: A National Call for Moral Revival.

May the fires of Pentecost burn bright again tonight.
May they purify our hearts for the battles ahead and scorch the blinders from our eyes.
May the Lord's holy fires alight upon the oppressive empire and make way for the kingdom of heaven on earth.
May a new church be born, a freedom church, which can speak good news to the poor.
The good news of the spirit, the precious breath, being held sacred for all of God's children.
The good news of rent canceled, a table prepared for us, a safe place to lay our heads, and healers' hands laid on all of us alike.
Amen.

BENEDICTION FOR HOMELESS PERSONS' MEMORIAL DAY

Prayer to a Homeless and Shivering God

Every year, cities across the United States hold services for the annual Homeless Persons' Memorial Day around December 21, the longest night of the year, or the winter solstice. This benediction was written by Rev. Lindsey Krinks for a service in Nashville. Krinks is the cofounder and director of advocacy at Open Table Nashville, an interfaith homeless outreach and advocacy nonprofit. She has worked on the streets of Nashville for nearly twenty years and is the author of Praying with Our Feet: Pursuing Justice and Healing on the Streets.

Homeless and shivering God,
God who weeps with us,
God by all the names we know you,
Stir our spirits now. Give us comfort, conviction, and courage as we face a new day, a new year, without these friends and loved ones by our side. May the spirits of our friends rest in peace in their new home where suffering is no more. And be with us as we go forward.

One: With the names of the dead on our lips,

All: We will go.

One: With hearts broken for those who don't survive the living hell of the streets,

All: We will go.

One: With the terrible knowledge of what happens to bodies that are denied health care and housing,

All: We will go.

One: With the secret sorrows we carry in our bones, with all the losses and grief,

All: We will go.

One: With the mysterious hope that death does not have the final say,

All: We will go.

One: With lives forever changed by those who have gone before us,

All: We will go.

One: With deep gratitude for friendship, community, and all those gathered around us today,

All: We will go.

One: With the great cloud of witnesses hovering around us,

All: We will go.

One: With the commitment to more daringly and lovingly embrace our neighbors,

All: We will go.

One: With the commitment to more compassionately tend the wounded in our midst,

All: We will go.

One: With the commitment to more courageously transform the broken systems around us,

All: We will go.

One: With the understanding that we will answer for hoarding our material possessions, wealth, and power for our own gain,

All: We will go.

One: With the commitment to leverage our resources, energy, and whatever relational and political capital we have to create a city that is more equitable and just,

All: We will go.

One: With the vision of a world where everyone has housing, health care, and hope,

All: We will go.

One: And with the dangerous belief that creating that world is possible,

All: We will go.

One: Go now to be the hands and feet of change.

Go now to embody the Beloved Community—the kin-dom of God—in the here and now.
Go now to re-member all who have been dis-membered in our society.
Go now in gentleness and fierceness to comfort the afflicted and afflict the comfortable.
Go now in the disruptive love that brings down the powerful from their thrones and lifts up the lowly.
Go now with the hot flames of hope in your hearts, letting your light shine into every crevice of darkness and injustice in this world.
Alone our lights flicker. Together we blaze.
Amen.

AN ANNIVERSARY RITUAL

A Ritual to Honor Our Past and Inspire Our Future

This ritual was adapted from the United Workers History Celebration during the twentieth anniversary of their organization in November 2022. Leaders of this ritual included Ashley Hufnagel, Michelle Rockwell, and Nadiyah Patterson. This ritual provides opportunities for reflection, connection, and forward-looking inspiration, anchoring participants in the history of an organization or community while also empowering them to carry its legacy into the future. 🌐

Materials Needed:

- Handout about the history of your organization or community
- Slide deck about your organization's history
- Organizational timeline
- Rocks
- Sample painted rocks
- Paint markers

Opening Session:

1. Breakfast Activity: Set up a table with rocks and paint markers during breakfast. Invite everyone to take a rock and write their name on one side.

2. Opening Mistica: Interactive Small Group Exercise & Ritual:

Explanation of Exercise: Distribute handouts of the years, events, and materials

- **Brief Slideshow of Your History:** Present a brief slideshow of key moments in your community or organization's history.
- **Pair Share:** Encourage attendees to find someone they don't know and share how and when they were introduced to your group.
- **Placing Rocks on Timeline:** After the pair share, invite participants to place their rocks on the spiral timeline.
- **Gather in Circle:** Form a circle around the timeline.
- **Short Discussion:** Facilitate a discussion about what is observed on the timeline.

Closing Session: Rock Circle

- **Finding Rocks and Writing:** Ask everyone to find their rock with their name and write one word on the flip side that describes something they are taking away from the assembly and want to carry into the year ahead.
- **Gathering in Circle:** Gather in a circle with the rocks.
- **Word Sharing:** One by one, each person shares their word, and the group repeats it in unison.
- **Closing Remarks:** Encourage participants to keep the rock as a souvenir, symbolizing what was created and accomplished during the weekend, the relationships built, the knowledge gained, and aspirations for leadership growth.

A PALM SUNDAY LITANY

A Litany of Hosanna and a Cry for Justice

Kelly Smith (leader in the New York State Poor People's Campaign and the Nonviolent Medicaid Army) and Rev. Dr. Jessica Williams wrote this litany for a Palm Sunday service with New York City churches, community leaders, NYC Poor People's Campaign leaders, and leaders from the Kairos Center in Washington Square Park, NY. All quotations taken from The Last Week: A Day-by-Day Account of Jesus's Final Week in Jerusalem *by Marcus J. Borg and John Dominic Crossan. We encourage you to augment the litany to include symbols of empire that exist in your city or town and find statistics about the conditions facing poor and low-income people in your state (see Fact Sheets on the Poor People's Campaign website).* 🌐

Reader 1: "Two processions entered Jerusalem on a spring day in the year 30. . . . One was a peasant procession, the other an imperial procession."

Reader 2: "These two processions embody the central conflict of the week that led to Jesus's crucifixion."

Reader 1: "Pilate's military procession was a demonstration of both Roman imperial power and Roman imperial theology."

Reader 2: Throughout the Roman Empire, imperial power and theology was displayed for all to see. One example was the Arch of Titus, constructed after the Great Revolt in Judea in which the Roman military killed over a million Jewish people and enslaved another hundred thousand. These atrocities were inscribed onto the arch. The Washington Square Triumphal Arch in New York City was designed to imitate the Arch of Titus, and serve as a reminder of empire, the imperial ideology on which this country was founded.

Reader 1: But we gather here today under this arch constructed to demonstrate military might, power, and theology to instead embody the subversive procession of the people made poor by empire, people impacted by systems of oppression as told in Matthew's gospel.

Reader 2: On this day which marks the beginning of Holy Week, we remember Jesus's counter-procession which "embodied not only a rival social order, but also a rival theology" and we lift up the lives of the 140 million poor and dispossessed people in this country today who suffer under conditions of poverty and state violence, like Jesus, his followers, and all those subjugated by the Roman Empire. Today this oppression under conditions of poverty, systemic racism, militarism and the war economy, and ecological devastation continues to be undergirded by a heretical theology of power. Like those who knew change was possible and laid down palms, exclaiming hosanna, this day we too, shout, "Hosanna, we cry justice!"

Reader 1: This day we embody a counter-procession of the people. When you hear us proclaim "it does not have to be this way" we invite you to respond with "Hosanna, we cry justice!" Let's try it: **"Hosanna, we cry justice!"**

Reader 2: Today we lament that a million New Yorkers will be thrown off of Medicaid on May 11. It does not have to be this way!

All: Hosanna, we cry justice!

Reader 1: We lament that 8.6 million New Yorkers (nearly half of us) are poor or low wealth. It doesn't have to be this way!

All: Hosanna, we cry justice!

Reader 2: We lament that seventy thousand people in New York City, the center of extreme power and wealth, are homeless. More than three thousand people live in the subways, streets, and parks. It does not have to be this way!

All: Hosanna, we cry justice!

Reader 1: We lament that 1.4 million New York City residents (nearly 17 percent) are food insecure and that one in three children in NYC are food insecure. It does not have to be this way!

All: Hosanna, we cry justice!

Reader 2: We invite those here to cry out, to proclaim the struggles and injustices that are hurting our people. [Pause and let folks shout out other struggles; have some planned.]

Reader 1: Just as Jesus and his disciples organized a counter-procession as part of a movement to bring social, political, economic, and spiritual transformation, today we too are organizing to build a moral movement to end poverty and its interlocking injustices, led by the poor.

Reader 2: We too know a revolution of values is needed that centers the voices of those most impacted. We too are building a movement to lift from the bottom so everybody rises.

Reader 1: We too shout, "Hosanna, we cry justice!" Join me!

All: Hosanna, we cry justice! Hosanna, we cry justice! Hosanna, we cry justice! Amen!

LAS POSADAS

A Litany for a Las Posadas Procession

In December 2022, Freedom Church of the Poor and La Iglesia del Pueblo hosted a Las Posadas procession with members of the East Harlem community at the People's Church in New York City. Traditionally a Latin American Catholic festival commemorating Mary and Joseph's search for lodging, this ritual was reinterpreted to highlight modern issues of poverty, displacement, and systemic injustice. Lasting nine nights from December 16 to Christmas Eve, the procession reflects on the historical and biblical journey of Mary and Joseph, who traveled for a census required to pay tribute to Rome. This journey, marked by economic hardship and denial of shelter, is paralleled with modern struggles against economic inequality, forced migration, and access to basic needs. Participants are encouraged to reflect on who the Josephs and Marys of today are. Who, in today's social and economic systems, is being displaced and denied their basic needs?

Overview

The procession will visit three to five key sites in the community, each representing important social justice issues. The final stop will be a welcoming place where attendees will share a meal and celebrate community.

Participants will dress as Joseph and Mary, carry instruments and candles, and hold signs supporting affordable housing, health care access, a just immigration system, fair wages, quality education, and more. 🌐

Sample Route and Stops

1. **First Stop: Luxury Apartment Building**
    - **Location:** Luxury apartment building that has displaced long-time residents.
    - **Purpose:** Highlight the right to affordable housing and the way poor and low-income people are being denied access to affordable housing.
    - **Testimonies:** A person experiencing housing insecurity and an advocate or housing policy expert.
    - **Closing Prayer:** "God of the poor, we have come looking for refuge, walk with us in our search for a better place—for your kingdom here on earth."
    - **Walk to Next Stop:** Sing the procession song and other seasonal songs.

2. **Second Stop: Local Hospital**
    - **Location:** Local hospital that serves the uninsured or publicly insured patients that is under threat of closure.
    - **Purpose:** Emphasize access to health care for all.
    - **Testimonies:** A patient who benefits from community health services and a health care provider or policy advocate, to speak about how a for-profit health care system is denying people access to health care.
    - **Closing Prayer:** "God of the poor, we have come looking for refuge, walk with us in our search for a better place—for your kingdom here on earth."
    - **Walk to Next Stop:** Sing the procession song and other seasonal songs.

3. **Third Stop: Immigration and Customs Enforcement Office or Detention Facility**

- **Location:** A facility where noncitizens are being detained while awaiting immigration proceedings or removal from the United States.
- **Purpose:** Advocate for a just immigration system.
- **Testimonies:** An immigrant sharing their journey and an immigration advocate or legal expert.
- **Closing Prayer:** "God of the poor, we have come looking for refuge, walk with us in our search for a better place—for your kingdom here on earth."
- **Walk to Next Stop:** Sing the procession song and other seasonal songs.

4. **Fourth Stop: Restaurant Franchise**
    - **Location:** Local restaurant chain that is exploiting workers.
    - **Purpose:** Highlight the need for fair wages and labor rights.
    - **Testimonies:** A worker advocating for fair wages and a labor rights activist or union representative.
    - **Closing Prayer:** "God of the poor, we have come looking for refuge, walk with us in our search for a better place—for your kingdom here on earth."
    - **Walk to Next Stop:** Sing the procession song and other seasonal songs.

5. **Final Stop: Community Center or Church**
    - **Location:** A welcoming community center, church, or similar venue.
    - **Purpose:** Celebrate the power of community and hope.
    - **Activities:** Share a meal, warm drinks, and fellowship.
    - **Opening Reflection:** "Upon arriving in Bethlehem of Judea, Joseph and Mary were desperately looking for a place to rest, they were hungry, tired, and their son was about to be born. They knocked on many doors . . . yet none welcomed

them in until finally, in a humble stable, they found the longed-for refuge. How many doors remain closed today for our poor communities, preventing their development, their health, their education, their freedom? What will be the place that will open their doors and become a beacon of light and hope in the midst of darkness this evening?"

  - **Final Testimony:** An inspiring story of community support and resilience.
  - **Closing Prayer:** "God of the poor, we have come looking for refuge, walk with us in our search for a better place—for your kingdom here on earth."

Additional Details

- **Weather Considerations:** Plan for possible cold or inclement weather by having warm clothing, portable heaters if necessary, and shelter options at each stop.
- **Song Sheet:** Distribute copies of the song sheet (see below).
- **Safety Measures:** Ensure there is a clear path for the procession, with safety marshals and first aid available.

By visiting these stops, the procession will not only highlight crucial social justice issues but also embody the spirit of community, care, and revolutionary hope.

Sample Song Sheet

OS PIDO POSADA
(Por CALEB—Venezuela)

Os pido posada
en nombre del cielo
Porque viene al mundo
nuestro redentor
Nuestro cuerpo espera
Un sitio de descanso
Solo hemos venido
por un lugar mejor.

I'M ASKING YOU FOR SHELTER
(By CALEB—Venezuela)

I'm asking you for shelter
in the name of heaven
Because our Redeemer
is coming to this world
Our body awaits
For a place to rest
We have only come
for a better place.

AN ASH WEDNESDAY RITUAL

Imposition of the Ashes

This ritual was part of a Freedom Church of the Poor Ash Wednesday service held at the Community Outreach Center at Asbury First United Methodist Church in Rochester, New York, in conjunction with the center's free breakfast, showers, laundry, and clothing programs. Those gathered include staff, guests, neighbors, volunteers, church members, and donors. It was written by Rev. Patrick Dupont, an ordained deacon in the United Methodist Church and the minister of outreach at Asbury First United Methodist Church in Rochester, where he is building a Freedom Church of the Poor community.

Portions of this liturgy are adapted from "A Service of Worship for Ash Wednesday."

Introduction

Leader:

It is a Christian tradition on Ash Wednesday to be marked with ashes as a sign that helps us remember that we are mortal and temporary on this Earth, that we are imperfect and make mistakes, and also as a visible sign of mourning over the deeply unjust state of the world around us. In a moment we will say a prayer together over the ashes and then play some music. While the music plays, I invite you to come forward and to receive ashes either on your forehead or on the back of your hand.

As we receive these ashes together, let us embody a spirit of lament.
Let us reflect on those places in our own lives where we struggle:
Those places where we feel we have made mistakes and have
a hard time letting ourselves off the hook and accepting
forgiveness,
but also those places in our lives where we fear that we, and
those we love, might be crushed by the oppressive forces of evil
and injustice in our world: poverty, oppression, racism, sexism,
military violence, ecological devastation . . .
Let us lament the state of our world,

A world that prioritizes profit over people,
that views extreme wealth and extreme poverty as necessary and natural,
that values power over equity,
that chooses war, violence, and coercion instead of life, compassion, and community,
A world of unfair rent hikes and evictions,
Of homelessness and hunger,
Of climbing costs and stagnant wages,
A world that is willing to sacrifice many for the sake of very few.
Let us call to mind and hold in prayer the places where we and our whole world are in desperate need of the liberating power of God.

There is a bit of a paradox built into Ash Wednesday: in accepting our own limitations and frailty and mortality, in acknowledging our own humanity and in facing the darkness head on, we come to a place where we realize that we actually might have nothing to lose . . . and we can be filled with the divine and swept up in that liberating love and power of God, becoming part of what the Rev. Dr. Martin Luther King Jr. called "a new and unsettling force," activated for the redemption and healing of this world for the sake of all who suffer.

Leader: Let us mourn injustice. Let us hope in liberation.

People: Let us mourn injustice. Let us hope in liberation.

Thanksgiving Over the Ashes

Leader: Will you join me in prayer?

People: Almighty God, you have created us out of the dust of the earth.

Grant that these ashes may be to us a sign of our mortality and penitence.

As we acknowledge our own humanity,

Let us recognize the shared humanity of all people.

As we make peace with our own mistakes and lament suffering and injustice in our world,

Let us remember your gracious gift of *life* and your imperative of *fullness of life* for all.

Amen.

Imposition of Ashes

*The leaders take their places in front of the congregation and invite the congregation to come forward. "I Am Not Afraid" (*Songs in the Key of Resistance: A Movement Songbook, *Song #18) is sung or played.* 🌐

The leaders dip a thumb in the ashes and make a cross on the forehead or hand of each person who chooses to come forward, saying to each,

> Remember that you are dust, and to dust you shall return.
> Repent, and embrace the good news of liberation.

Invitation to the Observance of Lenten Discipline/Call to Action

The following or similar words may be spoken:

The early Christians observed with great devotion the days of Jesus's passion and resurrection, and it became the custom of the Church that before the Easter celebration there should be a forty-day season of spiritual preparation.

As inheritors of this tradition, I invite you, in the name of the Freedom Church of the Poor, to observe a holy Lenten season of struggle and lament:

> by self-examination and repentance,
> by acknowledging and rejecting forces of evil in our world,

by engaging in rituals such as scripture reading, prayer and fasting,
by performing works of mercy, compassion, and justice,
by gathering people together to organize toward a more just future,
by embracing the liberating power of God at work in our lives and in our world.

You will see printed in your handouts, opportunities to further engage with Freedom Church of the Poor during this season. *[Here, leaders announce ways to connect to upcoming services, actions taking place, and petitions that people could sign.]*

Leader: Let us mourn injustice. Let us hope in liberation.

People: Let us mourn injustice. Let us hope in liberation.

All sing: "I Am Not Afraid."

LITANY OF REMEMBRANCE

A Prayer to Honor the Dead

Alex Zane, MDiv, a leader in the Freedom Church of the Poor, wrote this litany to honor the leadership of Anthony Williams and James Shearer during a Freedom Church of the Poor service in July 2023. Anthony and James were two longtime movement leaders who fought tirelessly for the rights of poor and homeless people. Williams was the cofounder of Picture the Homeless in New York City, an organization run and led by homeless and formerly homeless people. Their motto is, "Don't talk about us, talk with us." Shearer was the cofounder of Spare Change News, a street newspaper committed to putting a face on homelessness and helping to end homelessness. You can adapt the litany to honor the lives of people in your community who have died. 🌐

We the Freedom Church of the Poor grieve the passing of James Shearer and Anthony Williams.

In a land where poverty pushes our people to death, our grief cries out for justice.
We seek understanding by remembering them.
In the face of poverty, James and Anthony told the truth that there is more than enough for everyone to thrive.
In the face of racism, they declared equality.
In the face of militarism, they demanded peace.
In the face of ecological devastation, they brought healing.
In the face of white Christian nationalism, they lived as citizens of the world, faithful to the eternal Spirit of freedom.
Rather than be crushed by a wicked empire, their spirits danced with courage.
They shared their visions with us and showed a better way to live together.
And where there was hopelessness, they lit the light of hope.
We invite any who wish to speak a word about James or Anthony to do so.
[*Allow time for reflections.*]
Our beloved revolutionaries, James and Anthony, have joined the ancestors.
They live forever in a home of honor in our hearts.
We take up the good fight they fought, and when we rise, they rise with us.
Amen.

LITURGY FOR THE EARTH

A Ritual for Ecological Harmony and Justice

This ritual was offered by the Center for Earth Ethics at Union Theological Seminary for convocation, the start of the school year, on September 6, 2023. This liturgy was written by Karenna Gore, founder and executive director of the Center for Earth Ethics. Leaders from the Center—Gore,

Eugenia Cooper-Newton, Aja Two Crows, and Tory Field—facilitated this offering.

1. Prepare the Altar

Set an altar space that includes a bowl or bucket of water as well as an empty bowl or bucket, and two cups. Also include other elements on the altar: soil in a small shell or bowl, and fire (either a lit candle or an image of a flame or of the sun). The first part of the ritual will serve to honor the element of air, but you can also place something else on the altar to do so, such as a figure or drawing of a bird or a wind instrument like a harmonica or a whistle.

2. Opening Reflection

We begin with the words of Howard Thurman, the teacher of liberation and justice, a mentor to Dr. King, and the long-time dean of Rankin Chapel at Howard University and then Marsh Chapel at Boston University. He recalled the feeling he had as a child on the Atlantic coast of Florida: "I had the sense that all things, the sand, the sea, the stars, the night, and I were one lung through which all life breathed. Not only was I aware of the vast rhythm enveloping all, but I was a part of it, and it was a part of me."

Now as we begin this new time together, we call in and practice this insight. Close your eyes and breathe in and out, thinking of the rhythms of nature.

We have the elements of this Earth within each of our bodies: the air in our lungs; the iron in our blood; the water throughout, including in our mouth and eyes; the energy from the sunshine and soil in the food that sustains us.

3. Honoring the Air

We live in places within this living planet that are interconnected to other places, as if it was one body. The big ice at the poles, the lush forests in the Amazon and the Congo, the small islands in the middle of the vast oceans like those in the South Pacific, the deserts, the wetlands, the mountains, the valleys, all with peoples and other living beings, who are also breathing in and out as they live their lives there. We bring them to mind as we breathe.

We especially bring to mind those who are breathing contaminated air and dedicate our breath to being part of the movement to make it clean. We acknowledge that the air around the world is connected in that great expanse of sky that is like a protective layer around the Earth, the atmosphere. We bring to mind those who struggle to have the shelter and safety of a home in a stable climate. [Specific examples added as appropriate.]We dedicate our breath to the health of that vast expanse of the sky, and all that it contains.

We breathe as one with all life and dedicate our breath to remembering and protecting and taking good care of those most basic and essential elements of life—for all.

4. Honoring the Soil (Earth) and the Sun (Fire) and Water

We acknowledge that the food that nourishes us comes from other living beings that are meant to grow and thrive in good ways, drawing energy from sunshine and healthy soil and water as well as air. We bring to mind those that struggle for nourishing food and dedicate our breath to restoring their natural inheritance of sustenance from the Earth. We acknowledge and honor living bodies of water, and the water that comes from rainfall and from underground springs. We bring to mind those that struggle for clean water to drink and dedicate our breath to protecting the health of those waterways for their bodies and their lives.

5. Water Ritual and Offering to the Earth

Invite each person to come to the altar and take a small cup full of water from the full bowl and hold it and pray with it, or set intentions with mind and heart as they hold it. Then invite them to pour it into the empty bowl and hand it to the next person. If there is a large group, the second cup can be handed to someone to take some water before the person holding the first cup is finished. When everyone has had their turn, set the bowl that has been filled by their cups aside. Then move outside—or designate a smaller group of people to do so later—and pour it to the Earth as an offering. Share brief reflections. Close with a song or a prayer.

A POEM IN THE WAKE OF POLICE VIOLENCE

A Poem for Revolutionary Love

Tyre Nichols was fatally assaulted by Memphis police on January 7, 2023. This poem was written by Tony Eskridge, a leader with the Kairos Center from Memphis, Tennessee, who joined the protests after his murder. "Love Is, for Tyre" was first presented at the Kairos Center and the Labor-Religion Coalition of New York State's "Religion in a Time of Crisis" gathering in February 2023, at Broadway Presbyterian Church in New York City.

"Love Is, for Tyre"

I wanted to write a poem about love
and what it isn't,
but I always get lost in the dark.

I want to write a poem about love—
and what it is.

Love is safe,
that feeling you get when you're almost home.
It has long outstretched arms
big enough to hold you and me and all of us.

Love is community and
community is all of us.
The unhoused, the unfed, the unpaid—
we, the 140 million.

Love is water when you're thirsty
food when you're hungry
a room when you need a rest
a hand when you start to stumble
a family when you lose your sense of self.

Love is on the Bridge
between fear and the future
of a better world.
Between the evils that seek to control us
and a power that can unite us.
Love is on Poplar and Danny Thomas—
fists in the air with
sharpied shipping boxes.

Love is beautiful
and there is beauty all around us.
It's in the sky as the setting sun
casts a golden glow over our assembly.
It's in our actions and body aches
but there's still more to give.
It's with the skaters rolling down the hill
in unison to join us,
though there is someone missing.

Love is blasting Marvin Gaye and Juicy J
What's Goin On mane?
Love is in a pizza box, love is

in the hands that made it, the hands that gave it,
and the hands that ate it.

Love loves to get passed around.

Love is teaching my little friend how to catch
a frisbee. I tell her to look the other way—
flashing blue lights are blinding.
That was the last thing Tyre saw
before his life flashed.

Love is painful.
Where there is hate and fear, love is in pain.

To be violent and claim you love me
is a lie.
You cannot love and lie.
Don't lie to us when we see what you do
to people like us.

Love is the truth and the truth hurts,
but the truth will set us free.
Love is how we get free.

Love is active.
The time for love is right now.
We must cross that bridge together and
only together can we cross that bridge.
It is never too late to love.

Love is how we live.
Love is how we win.
Love is the light in the dark.

SONG OF HOPE

A Song to Counter Hate and Bring People Together

In January 2017, amid the division and hate-fueled rhetoric following Trump's presidency, Steff Reed wrote a song to bring people together around the universal value of love—a mantra that transcends politics, religion, and class. First sung at a New Orleans high school art exhibition on police brutality and anti-Blackness, the song offered hope as students united in its message. Steff Reed is a singer, songwriter, producer, and self-taught multi-instrumentalist who is currently pursuing a master's degree at Union Theological Seminary. 🌐

"Power of Love"

Verse 1
It's the match that sparks the flame
It's the action that inspires change
Power to the people in this holy war
And no weapon formed against it shall prosper.

Pre Hook
Hope and love can conquer anything
All you've gotta do is plant a seed of faith.

Hook
I believe in the power of love (2x's) Whoa—oh—oh—whoa (2x's)
I believe in the power of love.

Verse 2
It's liberation for everything
It's the reason the caged bird sings
It shines light, drives out the dark
It's the dream of freedom that Martin taught.

Pre Hook
Hook

Bridge
We're on a mission, fighting these conditions
The world is ours to live in and we can't let it fall
No bans, no borders. We're breaking down the wall
They can't divide us all if we believe.

Hook

SONG OF THE WATER PROTECTORS

A Song of Resistance, Healing, and Struggle Against Occupation

Te Martin is a community song leader, originally from Ramaytush Ohlone land in San Francisco. They wrote this song after being at Standing Rock for several months in 2016 to stand with Indigenous water protectors from over two hundred tribes to protest the construction of the Dakota Access Pipeline. Said Abdallah, a Palestinian friend of Te's, had joined the protests at Standing Rock and shared the connections he saw between the militarized violence at Standing Rock and the occupation of Palestine. He said that he wanted his "body to be a bridge for liberation of his Palestinian homelands." These words and the persistence of the water protectors at Standing Rock inspired this song. 🌐

May This Body Be a Bridge

May this body be a bridge
For the healing of this land
May the river flow through us
Cleansing greed from our hands.

We are, we are born from the water
We are, we are made from the land

Teach us, teach us oh Great Mother
To bring, to bring peace to this land.

A SHINNECOCK CALL FOR PEACE

A Song of Peace in a Death-Dealing Society

This song was written by Rev. Holly Haile Thompson of the Shinnecock Nation. It is deeply rooted in the lived experiences and reflections of the Shinnecock people and intersects other Indigenous communities and poor folks who must counter the violent, death-dealing practices of patriarchy, capitalism, and white supremacy. In March 2003, during a time of heightened global tension and imminent conflict, Rev. Holly led prayers for peace in two yoked neighboring non-Native congregations. Just three days later, the United States invaded Iraq. 🌐

Mothers and Children for Peace

Chorus [sing between verses]
You may not have, you may not have
You may not have my son
and smear his hands with blood
You may not have, you may not have
You may not have my daughter, dear,
and smear her heart with hate.

Verse 1
The plans for war, the thirst for blood
The cruel revenge is staged to prolong the fear
The thought of peace, the love of life
The vision of our children living side by side.

Verse 2
Time passes by, days filled with tears
Years languish on for all who lose their

dearest loved ones
My treasured child, not born to die
But born to live and lead us to the hope
that is tomorrow.

Verse 3
My sons and daughters, all growing children,
They will not kill for you, Makers of the Bombs!
My children breathe, their strong hearts beat
And they will teach us how we can live in Peace.

OM SHANTI SHANTI SHANTI

A Shiva Prayer to Ward Off Untimely Death

Sunita Viswanath, cofounder of the human rights organizations Women for Afghan Women, Sadhana: Coalition of Progressive Hindus, and Hindus for Human Rights, shared this prayer as part of a week-long hunger strike calling for a permanent ceasefire in front of the White House. This week of action was called to illustrate the policy of starvation that Israel's attack on Gaza was enforcing and was sponsored by Adalah Justice Project, the US Campaign for Palestinian Rights, Dream Defenders, Jewish Voice for Peace, the Kairos Center, and others.

At this time of so much death and conflict all around, I invoke the powerful Shiva prayer that Hindus chant to ward off untimely death. With the deaths of one thousand two hundred Israelis in the attack by Hamas, and the deaths of over fifteen thousand Palestinians in bombings by Israel that have targeted hospitals, refugee camps, UN shelters, schools, cities and villages, neighborhoods and homes, all I can do is scream for justice and pray for peace.

Om Tryambakam Yajamahe Sugandhim Pushtivardhanam/
urvarukamiva bandhanan mrityormuksheya mamritat

Om Shanti Shanti Shantihi
Om Peace Peace Peace
Om. We worship and adore you, O Three-Eyed One, O Shiva.
You are sweet gladness, the fragrance of life,
who nourishes us, restores our health, and causes us to thrive.
As, in due time, the stem of the plant weakens,
and the fruit is freed from the vine,
so free us from attachment and death, and do not withhold immortality.
Om Peace Peace Peace.

A GROUNDING PRAYER

A Prayer of Commitment to Social Justice

This grounding prayer was written by the Faith in Community Workgroup of Greater Birmingham Ministries in Birmingham, Alabama, and shared with the Freedom Church community by Rev. Carolyn Foster. Greater Birmingham Ministries (GBM) is a multifaith, multiracial organization that provides emergency services for people in need and engages the poor and the nonpoor in systemic change efforts. This prayer lifts up the mission of GBM to serve people, build community, and pursue justice.

O God of many names, remind us to love all people, no matter how hard we try to deny that love in our thoughts, words, and deeds.
Renew our hearts, our souls, and our bodies, so that we may serve people more fully.
Give us strength to stand with those who struggle, wisdom to see needs clearly, and courage to pursue justice.
Grant us compassion, so that we may open our arms, our minds, and our hearts to build community for all.
Amen.

A PRAYER FOR BLACK WOMEN AND GIRLS

Who Have Stood at the Dark End of the Street

In December 1662, the Virginia General Assembly passed a law stating, "Negro womens children to serve according to the condition of the mother," in response to Elizabeth Key's (an enslaved woman) 1656 lawsuit, where she won her freedom. This 1662 act served to prevent other enslaved people from gaining their freedom, legitimized the exploitation of enslaved women's bodies to sustain the labor force that built this nation's wealth, and further created a harmful narrative about Black women's bodies that persist today. The following prayer by Rev. Kym McNair honors all Black women and girls who have endured violence and control. Rev. McNair is the director of social transformation at My Sisters' Place (a domestic violence service organization located in Westchester County, New York) and organizer with the People's Institute for Survival and Beyond (a multiracial, multigenerational, movement-building organization based in New Orleans, Louisiana).

Dear God,

From the beginning of time, you have been and are still the proclaimer of justice. We cry out to you, the source of our strength and the strength of our lives! We call on you, the God who hears, to hear us now.

God Who Hears, hear us as we mourn for Black women and girls whose dreams were deferred and whose dignity was diminished due to violence against our bodies. We mourn for the lack of regard for the souls of your daughters made in your image. We lament for the lessons many of us learned too soon that we were not safe in a world full of men's unquenching desire for power, for knowing since we were little girls that our bodies were never ours alone.

Author of Life and Breath, we cry out to you on behalf Celia, Recy, Betty Jean, Rosa Lee, Marsha, and countless others whose voices were silenced by shameful actions outside of their control. For our sisters whose lives were taken willfully and in the terror of the night only for the sake of holding power.

RIGHTEOUS GOD, our anger is set on fire by the injustices we have had to suffer as we stand at the crossroads of racism and sexism. We rage at the complicity of people sworn to serve, protect, and do no harm. People who claim to know you as CREATOR OF ALL, but treat us as if they never met you and are silent to our pain.

LOVING GOD, we reject the lies told to us and about us generation after generation after generation that we are unloved and unlovable. We know we are fearfully, wonderfully, marvelously, and wondrously made in your image.

MOTHER OF WISDOM, we give thanks for Ida, Anna, Rosa, Fannie Lou, and countless others who raised their voices on behalf of their sisters. We raise our voices to join that righteous chorus!

SHE WHO IS STRENGTH, we who believe in freedom, justice and liberation for Black women and girls will not rest until the lives of your daughters is as important as the lives of the rest of your children and the dangers at the end of the street are no more. Give us the strength we need for the coming of the days when our voices are heard and our lives are protected.

Note: The names of God come from Rev. Dr. Wilda Gafney's *Women's Lectionary for the Whole Church* series.

The women listed:
Celia (no known last name)
Recy Taylor
Betty Jean Owens

Rosa Lee Coates
Marsha P. Johnson
Ida B. Wells
Anna Julia Cooper
Rosa Parks
Fannie Lou Hamer

A PRAYER FOR DIWALI

A Prayer for Light in Times of Darkness

Diwali is a holiday celebrated by millions of Hindus around the world. It involves the worship of the goddess Lakshmi (Laxmi). *According to the creation myth of the* Samudra Manthan, *Lakshmi is one of the goddesses who emerges during the churning of the cosmic ocean. Lakshmi is celebrated as the goddess of wealth, but what she represents is far more than material wealth. Her four hands represent* artha, dharma, kama, *and* moksha: *material well-being, morality, love, and liberation. These four aspects are inseparable in Lakshmi. That is, well-being, morality, love, and liberation are indivisible. Lakshmi reveals to us a world that is possible if we understand the four aspects as a whole. This prayer is written by Shailly Gupta Barnes, the policy director of the Kairos Center in New York City. Barnes has used her background in law, economics, and human rights to work with and for dispossessed communities for nearly twenty years.* 🌐

A Prayer for Diwali

Om Jai Lakshmi
Goddess born from the struggle between good and evil
Guide us toward the light.
In a world where plenty is possible,
Let us end hunger, thirst, and homelessness.

In your nurturing hands,
Let us seek refuge from want, fear, and violence.
With your grace,
Let our world be reborn in your image,
Where all needs are met,
Where morality and love are abundant,
And whereby we are free.
Om Jai Lakshmi.
Om Shanti, Shanti, Shanti.

A PRAYER FOR DEMOCRACY

A Prayer of Moral Resistance

On Inauguration Day 2017, Rev. Dr. Liz Theoharis helped lead the National Prayer Call for Hope and Focus as part of a Day of Moral Resistance, along with Repairers of the Breach.

God of justice and righteousness, we come to you seeking justice, dignity, and prosperity for all.

As Rev. Dr. King said in the last year of his life: We live in a cruelly unjust society. In a world where, on Dr. King's birthday, just a few days ago, Oxfam can come out with a report that exposes that eight people own and control as much wealth as half the world's population, we know that this is not just, that this is not your will being done.

Earlier today, a political leader was sworn in as the president of the United States. A preacher compared this leader to Nehemiah from the holy Bible. But we know that you shuddered when you heard this, God. Nehemiah helped to rebuild his society after it was destroyed by poverty, slavery, conquest, and war;

Nehemiah wasn't responsible for and didn't benefit from poverty, discrimination, and war. And when your prophet Nehemiah rebuilt Jerusalem, restored the streets so that the people could live in them; he did not separate and deport families, or cut people off from health care. He didn't privatize their children's education or refuse to pay the laborers living wages. He put the needs of the least of these who are most of us at the heart of the city—at the heart of the society—because the poor, the immigrants, the women, the LGBTQ people are the heart of God.

In these difficult days ahead of us we can take encouragement from Walter Rauschenbusch, the great social gospel preacher, who challenged the robber barons and bigots and pharaohs of his day, and his *Prayers of the Social Awakening*. He prayed as we pray now:

> We bless thee for the inspired souls of all ages who saw afar the shining city of God, and by faith left the profit of the present to follow their vision. Make us determined to live by truth and not by lies, to found our common life on the eternal foundations of righteousness and love, and no longer to prop the tottering house of wrong by legalized cruelty and force. Help us make the welfare of all, the supreme law of the land, so that our commonwealth may be built strong and secure, on the love of all its inhabitants. Cast down the throne of Mammon who ever grinds the lives of women and men, and set up your throne, O God. Show your erring children at last the way from the City of Destruction to the City of Love, and fulfill the longing of the prophets of humanity. Our God, once more we make thy faith our prayer: "Thy kingdom come! Thy will be done on earth!"

May we make it so. May we work for justice. May we march tomorrow and every day until justice comes. In your many names of justice and righteousness, we pray, Amen.

A PRAYER FOR A CITY OR TOWN

A Prayer for a Local Council Meeting

Rev. Lindsey Krinks is the cofounder and director of advocacy at Open Table Nashville, an interfaith homeless outreach and advocacy nonprofit. She has worked on the streets of Nashville for nearly twenty years and is the author of Praying with Our Feet: Pursuing Justice and Healing on the Streets. *This prayer served as the opening prayer for a Metro Council meeting in Nashville, Tennessee, in 2017.*

God of the Disinherited, God of the Laborer, God of All People,
Many of us in this room will go home tonight
to sleep safely in our beds with full bellies
while thousands of our neighbors are huddled beneath bridges,
hidden in alleys, missions, and jails,
unsure of what tomorrow will bring.
I pray that you, O God, would remind us that all those suffering
are part of our community, our family, our body.
Remind us that our liberation is bound up
with the liberation of all those who are cast out.
God, as our city is being bought by the highest bidder,
I pray that you would bring conviction and courage
to our leaders.
Help us all to set aside petty grievances and vain ambitions
and work for the common good of all our people.
God, let us not be rich while others are destitute,
nor be in good health if we do not tend the wounds
of those without care.
Let our city not enjoy peace until we have justice.
Let us not wave the flag of unity until we have equity.
Let us not boast about our diversity
while the gods of white supremacy
are still seated in the halls of power.
God, we pray that all those who labor would find rest,

and that all those who benefit from exploiting that labor
would be stirred with a restlessness for justice.
We pray that all those who are excluded
from being full members of our community
would find protection and radical inclusion.
We pray that those who misuse power
would be held accountable.
And we pray that all those who are working for justice,
in this room and beyond,
would find strength, support, and solidarity.
Forgive us our trespasses, O God,
and fill us with your spirit of love—
a love that is as disruptive as it is healing.
Teach us what it looks like, feels like, and sounds like
to bring good news to the poor,
release to the captives,
and freedom to the oppressed in Nashville.
We pray these things in the name of the God of Disruptive Love,
Amen.

A PRAYER FOR BLACK AUGUST

Prayers for the People

This prayer was written by Pastor Wesley Morris for a Black August Freedom Church of the Poor service organized by the Kairos Center, Donkeysaddle Projects, the Highlander Research and Education Center, and the Dream Defenders SunDDAy School. Black August began in California's prisons in the 1970s after the deaths of Jonathan and George Jackson and other Black prisoners seeking freedom. It now commemorates organizations and revolutionaries targeted by the American state and prepares developing leaders for future struggle. In August 2023, we commemorated Black August with Freedom Church of the Poor sessions focused on the Watts Uprising, the 1968 Poor People's Campaign, the

National Welfare Rights Organization, the original Rainbow Coalition, Black veterans, the March on Washington, the League of Revolutionary Black Workers, and more. Morris, the senior pastor of Faith Community Church in Greensboro, North Carolina, has worked with the Beloved Community Center of Greensboro, home of the nation's first "Community Truth and Reconciliation Process," for over a decade.

Dear God, we offer the prayers of the people today in honor of Black August and in honor of Black life and the movement of unity—unifying our people, even across distance and difference.

I lift up this prayer in their honor.

We pray for your holy church that is within and beyond our freedom dreams
And within and beyond our most sincere practices
As we keep revolution constantly on our mind
In our respective material and spiritual homes
Grant that every member of your discipleship church may truly and humbly use what we have to make your hope more glorified
And that our beloved bonds between each other will be more well known.

We pray for a fresh anointing of leadership
For gatherers, teachers, friends, repairers, seeders, menders, welcomers, and Black lovers in Black August.
We pray for all those who harness responsibility and work hours unknown
Who breathe their way through moments of disregard and tie their shoes with determination.

Oh God, forgive us for timidity in the face of wrongdoing.
Grant us compassion in the face of our fears as we overcome them one by one.

Give us the grace of time as we learn to do your will in each endeavor we undertake.

Oh God, have compassion on those who suffer from any grief, pain or trouble.

In the names that are being lifted up by other prayers being spoken right now, and those that are lifted up in silence.

And we even name ourselves.

Giving to the departed their eternal rest, we praise you for those saints who we have come into contact with and have had the honor to share presence and space.
May your light perpetually shine upon them so we can remember.
Let us now pray for our own needs and those of others
That we might not only build up our own selves, but build up our neighbors
Might not it be one's own materials, but they be *our* materials.

In the spirit of the words that were spoken before me
When we say amen, might it be that we maintain unity thereafter.
Amen.

A PRAYER FOR HEALING

A Prayer to Heal Our Hearts, Our Streets, and Our World

Shane Claiborne delivered this prayer as an invocation at a December 2017 Philadelphia City Council meeting. Claiborne is an evangelical Christian leader, author, and founding member of The Simple Way, a nonprofit organization in Philadelphia. He is also a cofounder of Red Letter Christians and a social activist known for his advocacy of nonviolence and service to the poor.

Dear God—
Thank you for creating a perfect world.
Forgive us for the mess we have made of it.
We pray for those who are suffering today.

We remember all those who suffer from violence.
The sin that goes all the way back to Cain and Abel. Where the blood cries out to you from the ground.
We remember the lives lost—the Natives, the enslaved.
Heal the wounds of history.

We remember all the lives lost.
Trayvon Martin. Michael Brown. Sandra Bland. Tamir Rice. Freddie Gray. Eric Garner. Anthony Smith.
You know their names. Each a precious child of yours.
Have mercy on us.

We remember those seeking refuge today.
You said to welcome the foreigner as if they were our own flesh and blood for we were once foreigners in the land of Egypt.
We pray—For immigrants and refugees.
Women, men, children.
For the victims of war and persecution.
For the addicted.
For the homeless.
For the imprisoned and the tortured.
For the widows and the orphans. Give us compassion.
We know that when we welcome them, we welcome you.

Heal our hearts,
Lord. Forgive us . . .
For choosing ourselves over others.
For prioritizing the rich over the poor.
For turning others into enemies.
For trusting in the sword more than the cross.

For disrespecting the earth.
For creating a world where so many have so little . . . and so few have so much.
For building prisons rather than schools
And building walls instead of bridges.
For forgetting the most vulnerable among us. Forgive us.

Deliver us O God.
Deliver us from the tyranny of greed, and pride, and power.
Deliver us from the contagion of fear.
From the myth of redemptive violence.
From addiction to control. From the seduction of wealth.
Deliver us, from the idolatry of nationalism.
The ugliness of racism. The cancer of hatred.
The paralysis of cynicism.
The violence of our silence. Deliver us.
From the ghettos of poverty. And the ghettos of wealth.
Deliver us from ourselves.

I pray for these leaders of our city, O God.
Break their hearts with the things that break yours.
Give them eyes to see those on the margins.
Give them courage to overcome evil with good.
Help them to disagree well, and look for the truth where they might least expect to find it.
Give them imagination that they might think outside the box.
Give them a vision for justice that is big enough to heal both the oppressed and the oppressors.
Give them compassion for our most vulnerable citizens.
Let them be driven by love not by fear.

Give us dreams and visions . . . for our city. And for our world.
Dreams of your upside-down kingdom where the last are first and the first are last,

Where the mighty are cast from their thrones and the lowly are lifted up,
Where the poor are blessed, and the peacemakers are the children of God.
Where we beat our weapons into farm tools and study violence no more. And where every person has "this day their daily bread."

Make this a City of Love.
Where all are welcome . . . no matter who they are or where they come from.

I pray all this in the name of the God of infinite hospitality who welcomes us all.
The God who was born a refugee in a manger and died executed on a cross, who knows our suffering and is near to those with broken hearts: Jesus.

Amen.

A REVOLUTIONARY ADVENT WREATH

An Advent Ritual

This ritual was co-created during Advent 2023 with the Freedom Church of the Poor community. Groups from across the country, including the Southern Tier Freedom Church, La Iglesia del Pueblo in NYC, the Open Table Kansas City, and the National Union of the Homeless, met virtually each Sunday. Becca Forsyth of Elmira, New York, a leader with the Poor People's Campaign and the Freedom Church of the Poor, helped to develop and lead this revolutionary Advent wreath ritual. 🌐

Introduction

Reader 1: As we travel through the season that Freedom Church knows as the Advent of a Revolution, we prepare our hearts and minds for the spark of a transforming change in this world. As we commemorate the two-thousand-year-old story of a brown-skinned, Palestinian, Jewish carpenter who brought the light that changed the world, we do not squander this space with performative gestures but rather we focus our energy on the flame that dwells within each of us and the power of these flames roaring together to bring peace and justice to this world. We feel the tension in the air, we see the battles raging, we hear our brothers and sisters crying out for air, food, shelter, and life itself. We come together and cry out for justice!

Reader 2: In this new ritual of the Revolutionary Advent wreath, each week, we will light our Advent candles to contemplate the four pillars of Advent: hope, peace, joy, and love. As we light the candle, we offer a prayer from the book *We Cry Justice: Reading the Bible with the Poor People's Campaign*, to reflect on these topics. And each week, we will invite a social justice organization/community to lead these prayers. And each week, participants will be invited to add images and thoughts that represent each pillar of Advent to our physical or virtual altar.

Week 1: Hope

> Creator, grant us the spirit of the persistent widow and all those who, when their backs are against the wall, persist for justice in spite of their plight. And most loving God, encompass all of these movements in your embrace and enable us all to dedicate ourselves to preaching, teaching, and spreading the good news: the news of Hope! Amen!
>
> —Erica Williams and Aaron Scott

Prompt: On the first Sunday of Advent the Hope candle is lit. What are the ways you see hope manifested in our collective work for justice? [*People are invited to offer words, phrases, images, and slogans that evoke hope in their life and add them to the altar.*]

Reflect: As we consider the presence of hope in our collective work for justice, we are encouraged to reflect on how we can embody and spread hope through our work to build unity, collective power, and solidarity across our states and around the world.

Week 2: Peace

> God, in the same way you guided Maria and Jose in their migration journeys to Bethlehem, we ask you to guide the journeys of all migrants and refugees who are currently crossing borders to have a better life. Help us liberate ourselves from the tyrants who, like Herod, misuse their power and position to oppress us. Guide our movement to end poverty, systemic racism, ecological devastation, and the war economy. We ask you to give us the strength of Maria and Jose to embrace this task, for it is through your son, Jesucristo, that we learn to stand up to Empire. Amen.
>
> —Kenia Torres-Alcocer

Prompt: On the second Sunday of Advent, the Peace candle is lit. What are the ways you see peace manifested in our collective work for justice? [*People are invited to offer words, phrases, images, and slogans that evoke peace in their life and add them to the altar.*]

Reflect: Peace is not merely an absence but requires the presence of justice. In a world that is divided by fear and hatred, we embody peace when we welcome the migrant and show hospitality to the stranger. In building deep solidarity across historical lines of division, we demonstrate our belief in the worth and dignity of every individual and help to bring about true and lasting peace in this world.

Week 3: Joy

> God, your miracles surround us. Guide us in fulfilling your will that we may live together in equality, sharing your abundance. With overflowing joy, we give ourselves to you and to each other.

> We give out of our poverty to support each other as we organize together for justice. Give us such grace today and every day. Amen.
>
> —Colleen Wessel McCoy

Prompt: On the third Sunday of Advent, the Joy candle is lit. What are the ways you see joy manifested in our collective work for justice? [*People are invited to offer words, phrases, images, and slogans that evoke joy in their life and add them to the altar.*]

Reflect: As we reflect on the joy in our collective work for justice, we are reminded not only to reflect on the sources of joy in our individual lives but also to consider how we can be conduits of joy for others. Let us be reminded that God is a God of abundance who calls us to look beyond our own needs and desires and to help build a world where all people can thrive.

Week 4: Love

> Let us believe in a God who identifies with the least of these. A God of love and of abundant life who stands on the side of justice. A God who is with us in the fields of Immokalee, in the tent encampments of the unhoused in Aberdeen, and with the mothers in Flint without clean water. A God who walks with us on the picket lines and in our organizing work. Let us remember the strength and love of those unsung saints of yesterday and today who resist and lead us all to freedom. Amen.
>
> —Rev. Dr. Liz Theoharis

Prompt: On the fourth Sunday of Advent, the Love candle is lit. What are the ways you see love manifested in our collective work for justice? [*People are invited to offer words, phrases, images, and slogans that evoke love in their life and add them to the altar.*]

Reflect: Advent is a time to remember that God is with us—in places of struggle, suffering, and resilience. As we face overwhelming challenges all around us, let us remember that when we embrace God's love, we too have a deep capacity for love and resilience that can pave the way for a more just and peaceful world.

A BLESSING FOR PEACE AND RESISTANCE

A Ritual for Life

This ritual was offered during the Kairos Center's Fall 2023 Minister's Training as part of a session on Building the Freedom Church of the Poor: Ritual, Worship + Liturgies. In the wake of devastating Israeli bombings and the tragic loss of Palestinian lives following the Hamas attacks on October 7, this ritual developed to honor the humanity and sacredness of life in the face of violence and death. The ritual was created and carried out by Rev. Chad Collins, Dr. Charon Hribar, Ciara Taylor, Rev. Erica Williams, Rev. Dr. Letiah Fraser, and Rev. West McNeill. The ritual opened with Rafeef Ziadah's poem, "We Teach Life, Sir" and closed with Te Martin's song, "May This Body Be a Bridge." 🌐

Materials Needed: Olive Oil (or Alternative Oil)

Leader 1: As we gather today, we want to remind ourselves that an important thing about ritual is that it creates in us the world we want to see.

Olives and olive branches and olive oils have deep meaning and have been used for ritual for generations. Olives and the olive branch have been symbols of peace and how much we need peace in our world, in our country, and in our lives right now.

Olive oil is a symbol of life and the divine presence that is in us, each of us, and around us. Oil was used in the ancient world to anoint kings, and when the unnamed woman anointed Jesus in Bethany, the house of the poor. Jesus himself was poor and living under imperial rule and facing crucifixion at the hands of the empire.

In this context, the act of the unnamed woman who anointed Jesus became an act of resistance.

It was a rejection of the rules of empire, and it was an act to lift up Jesus, a poor person, leading a social movement that would bring good news to the poor, release to the prisoners, sight to the blind, and liberation to the oppressed.

This oil that we hold in our hands is powerful because each of us is powerful.

Leader 2 (Blessing of Our Hands): I want to invite us to bring our attention to our hands. Our hands are strong, and they're vulnerable. They're powerful, and they're delicate. Our bodies have an incredible ability to heal and to repair. And yet are also so fragile. We all will one day return to the ground from which we came. And this basic truth of our humanity ties us all together. I want to invite you, if you have some oil with you, to anoint your hands with oil.

May we remember our embodiedness with gratitude and humility.
May we remember our intrinsic connection to every other body on this earth.
May we hold each other fiercely with love through all that this short life brings.

Leader 3 (Blessing of Our Heads): Family, with the oil on your hands, I invite you to close your eyes if you are comfortable doing so. Take your hands and place them on your head or your face, feel your head, feel your face. Remember that you, like every other human being, have been made in the holy image of God.

Precious God, we cry out to you as we touch and we feel our very face, the ones that resemble you, Lord. You created the whole world, but you made us to resemble you. In your image, we were made.

We thank you for that gift. We thank you, Lord, for the knowledge that you've given us over these years that we have grown to understand that each and every human being looks like you, made in your holy image.

As we are grateful for that knowledge, Lord, we break inside for the lack of care, the lack of love, and the disregard for your image bearers.

We lament that so many of our political leaders are living and leading with such disregard for your image bearers.

We honor those bodies made in your image that have been slaughtered, those bodies who are wounded, those bodies without water, without life's most basic needs.

As hard as it is for us, oh God, we lift those image bearers who have the power in their hands to do what's right and to honor your image, to honor and fight for and provide for each child, mother, and father.

Oh God, we cry out, Lord, that those who bear your image, which is all of us, would see you in everyone that we lay our eyes on.

We pray especially, oh God, that you change the eyes of our leaders.

Leader 4 (Blessing of Our Lips and Our Feet): Spirit of the living God, we come before you at this time asking for you to anoint our lips and our feet afresh.

Spirit of the living God, give us lips that will speak truth and not tell lies to continue the hate that is spreading all over this land.

Oh Spirit, touch our feet so that we don't run away from injustice, but we run toward it, knowing that we are covered on every side and that God, you are with us, even in the midst of terror, God, you are with us

We will stand strong in your strength, oh God, because we recognize it is not by power nor by might, but by your spirit.

So fill us up again, oh God. Fill our lips with words that will bring healing to the land.

Fill us up, oh God, that our lips will speak forth truth, righteousness, and justice.

Oh God, we need you right now. Fill us, oh God, from the very top of our heads to the bottom of our feet.

Let us be carriers of the gospel. The gospel of the revolutionary, brown-skinned, Palestinian Jew who made it very clear that he didn't come to be status quo.

He wasn't a chaplain of the empire but a prophet of God.

Let us be the lips and the feet that you are calling for in this hour, not ashamed, not afraid, and not shrinking back.

But let us go forward boldly knowing that we, we are the ones, oh God, that you are calling for in this moment, not those of past or those to come. But right now we are the prophets of a destiny that is not our own.

Let us remember, God, that we are vessels. Vessels of love, vessels of light, vessels of liberation called in this dark world to bring forth justice and healing.

We thank you right now for doing it. We thank you right now for strengthening us.

And we thank you right now, for although it may seem dark, oh God, you have shown us many times that we, the people together, if we sing together, if we march together, oh God, that we can win.

And so we stand strong in the belief, oh God, that even though we may be in darkness right now, God, that light is coming and that we will be those who stand on the side of light, truth, and justice.

It's in every name that is holy. I pray this prayer with great faith and expectation. Ashe. Amen. And blessed be.

A PRAYER TO END POVERTY

A Ritual of Breath and Power

This ritual prayer was written and delivered by Cedar Monroe in Olympia, Washington, for the Poor People's Campaign: A National Call for Moral Revival's Mass Poor People's and Low-Wage Workers' Simultaneous State House Assemblies.

Thank you all for being here. I want to ask you all to take a moment and to take a deep breath.

As you breathe in, imagine that you are drawing energy from the roots of the earth beneath you. And as you breathe out, imagine you are releasing that energy in the earth above you.

I want you to feel your power.

I want you to feel our power together.

We stand here today in a broken and divided land. 168 years ago, the United States government subjugated the Indigenous people of this land in the Puget Sound war, forcing Indigenous people onto reservations, killing and starving many, robbing people of their language and land and culture. It saw this land as a resource, and for the last 168 years, big business has made billions on billions on its water and its trees, destroying whole ecosystems and replacing what was once rich human life with the land with concrete and asphalt and suburbs.

Is it any wonder that a society built on that horrific act stands now on the brink of catastrophe? Is it any wonder we stand here today wrestling with poverty, systemic racism, environmental destruction, and a military machine that even now is bombing Gaza, that is enacting yet another genocide against yet another Indigenous people? Is it any wonder that we live in a morally bankrupt society that is turning to even more extreme white Christian nationalism?

So I want you to breathe again.

As you breathe in, imagine that you are drawing energy from the roots of the earth beneath you. And as you breathe out, imagine you are releasing that energy in the earth above you.

I want you to feel your power.

I want you to feel our power together.

Every one of us stands right now on land that has power. All around us, the earth itself is rebelling against the capitalism and colonialism and imperialism and death brought by Western powers. Fossil fuel and industry have changed the earth: the sea is rising, the earth is warming, and the weather is changing drastically, and I'm not saying that we will all survive it. But the earth is alive, and it is fighting for life, and it is more powerful than the handful of greedy white men ruling the world at the moment. The Indigenous people of this land are here too, after centuries of death and destruction, and they too are fighting for this land and its healing.

And every one of you has ancestors who, at least at one time, maybe a very, very long time ago, were connected with the land, wherever they were from. And understood how it worked. And revered it.

So I want you to breathe again.

This time, as you breathe in, I want you to call on your ancestors. Any ancestors, chosen or biological, who help guide your life. Ancestors that were once or still are connected to the land.

As you breathe out, I want you to send them out to stand with us today.

I want you to feel your power.

I want you to feel our power together, seen and unseen.

So now, here we are. We are homeless. We are denied health care. We experience police violence and state violence and incarceration. We can't get decent jobs, and we can't pay our rent, and our wages are not keeping up with inflation, and we don't know how we are going to feed our families. Our people are dying from disease induced by pollution, and nothing is done to address the climate change that will damage each of our communities, some beyond repair. All of these realities are felt even in the poor white communities I am from, but Indigenous and Black and brown communities experience them at even higher rates, along with constant racism and hatred at every level of society. Queer people and trans people, we are also being targeted. We are in a particularly dangerous moment when white Christian nationalism gains power; they are trying to roll back all the gains of the civil rights movement.

And we are facing an election that makes us feel helpless, because there are no candidates that are even addressing our plight. In this moment, capitalism and colonialism and imperialism have the upper hand. They are winning. We feel helpless in this moment. They have all the power. And so many people are dying because of it.

So I want you to breathe again.

As you breathe in, imagine that you are drawing power, power from the earth, from each other, from your ancestors. And as you breathe out, imagine you are releasing that power into this space.

I want you to feel your power.

I want you to feel our power together.

Just a few short years before the Civil War, Fredrick Douglass gave a speech, painting that moment as one of the darkest moments he and the movements against slavery had ever faced, just after the Dred Scott decision. He said, "Oppression, organized as ours is, will appear invincible up to the very hour of its fall." Perhaps we are at a similar moment today.

We are watching the powers that created these systems of oppression double down on the power they have left, which is considerable.

But empires never last. This land, right here, remembers a better way. The earth is fighting for life with you. All over the world, poor people are rising up and fighting back. You are part of a long fight against this system of greed that has overtaken our world, but it can't last forever. You will do your part; we will do our part. Surrounded by each other, by the earth, by our good ancestors.

So I want you to breathe a final time. Whatever your faith tradition, whoever the god or spirit or gods or ancestors or force you call on, if you do, call on them now.

As you breathe in, imagine that you are drawing power, power from them, from the earth, from each other, from your ancestors. And as you breathe out, hold that power close to your heart.

Hold on to it when it seems like the oppressors are winning. Hold on to it when you feel despair. Hold on to it when you watch the news and when you are treated unfairly. Hold on to it.

That power will win out in the end.

Let it be so.

A GROUNDING MEDITATION IN A TIME OF GENOCIDE

A Grounding Meditation

This grounding meditation was offered by Nubia Chong (she/her) as part of a healing and reflection space for community leaders and organizers on the frontlines of #CeasefireNow actions in the Fall of 2023 calling for United States leaders to demand an immediate ceasefire in Gaza and full liberation of the Palestinian people. Nubia is a trauma attuned psychiatrist and therapist, intuitive somatics educator/facilitator, and organizer with Freedom Healers DC. She believes in building collective resilience through community and embodiment. She is part of a circle of clergy and healers who support organizers and community leaders protesting the occupation and genocide in Palestine.

I pause to create sacred space for my grief and rage,
I locate the grief and rage in my body,
I stay with and bear witness to the sensations that arise.
I honor the sensations and ask my body what it might need to feel cared for in this moment.
I lovingly care for my body in the way it needs so I may be of service to this movement for liberation and justice.

Gentle Reminder: Violence surrounding us activates our survival responses. We must lovingly care for ourselves to prevent exhaustion from toxic stress. We must keep taking action in the way we know best. Meaningful action softens the feeling of powerlessness, softens the trauma responses, and allows energy to move through. May we find ways to alchemize our collective rage, grief, and terror into collective action demanding the liberation and safety of the people in Gaza.

A BLACK FRIDAY PRAYER FOR WORKER JUSTICE

A Thanksgiving Prayer and Call to Action

This prayer was written by faith leaders in support of Organization United for Respect at Walmart (OUR Walmart) as they prepared actions for Black Friday 2016 to back Walmart strikers and workers. As the nation's largest employer, with 1.3 million employees, Walmart sets the standard for the low-wage economy, promoting part-time, unpredictable work that becomes the norm if unchallenged. Walmart workers and community leaders united to improve working conditions, raise wages, and demand respect and dignity. This prayer is suitable for sharing on Thanksgiving Day.

Spirit of Life/Most Divine/God/Beloved Community/Creator,

We give thanks. We give thanks for those of us gathered at the table. We give thanks to those who bring us this day our food. We give thanks for the food farmers and workers collected. We give thanks for the hands who helped set this table: factory workers, construction workers, truck drivers, mechanics, stock people, cashiers, managers.

This Black Friday, we remember that we are not replaceable, we are priceless. We remember community and compassion can see us through the coming winter, storms, and tribulations. We remember we are blessed to have each other after ages of struggle.

You are a God of compassion and justice who has taught us to pursue a more just and sacred society, built upon foundations of fairness and love. As we enjoy this delicious meal surrounded by loved ones and dear friends, we turn our hearts inward to you this Thanksgiving, oh God, with thanks for the blessings you have bestowed upon us, so evident here on this special day.

And we lift up Walmart workers and other low-wage workers in our nation all days, but especially tonight and tomorrow as they claim their voice. We join our voice to theirs; they remind us of all that we are and all that we fight for. We give them our thanks, our love, and our support.

Amen.

AN INTERFAITH LITANY

A Litany of Moral Revival

This litany was written for the launch event of the Poor People's Campaign: A National Call for Moral Revival in Washington, DC, December 4, 2017, by the Rev. Dr. Jessica Williams and Dr. Charon Hribar, two longtime leaders of the Kairos Center. Interfaith leaders and community leaders from struggles of the poor and dispossessed around the country participated in the reading.

Reader 1: Today we stand as truth tellers witnessing the pain and suffering caused by the injustices within our community and across this country. We gather to declare that we need a moral revival, a radical revolution of values. And we call on the prophets of old from the sacred texts of the world's religions who proclaimed:

Reader 2: "The believers, both men and women are in charge of and responsible for one another; they all enjoin the doing of what is right and forbid the doing of what is wrong . . ." (Qur'an 9:71).

Reader 3: "All the workers you've exploited and cheated cry out for judgment. The groans of the workers you used and abused are a roar in the ears of God," (James 5:4).

Reader 4: "Arjuna, whenever righteousness is on the decline, unrighteousness is in the ascendant, then I am reincarnated. For the protection of the virtuous, for the extirpation of the evildoers, and for establishing Dharma [righteousness] on a firm footing, I am born from age to age" (Bhagavad Gita 4:7-8).

Reader 5: We uphold our Constitution and the founding creed of our Nation. "We hold these truths to be self-evident, that all men [and women] are created equal, that they are endowed by their Creator with certain unalienable Rights, that among these are Life, Liberty, and the Pursuit of Happiness," (Declaration of Independence).

Reader 1: Fifty years ago, Rev. Dr. King said, "There comes a time when silence is betrayal. The truth must be told."

All Voices: We are here. We are ready. We will break the silence.

Reader 6: The truth is that half the United States is poor or low-income, and that more than two hundred and fifty thousand people die each year from poverty, the lack of education, and the lack of health care, and thousands more from the denial of Medicaid expansion.

All Voices: We are here. We are ready. We will break the silence.

Reader 2: "The most urgent, the most disgraceful, the most shameful, and the most tragic problem is silence."—Rabbi Joachim Prinz.

Reader 4: We must break the silence of systemic racism in our society. We must speak out against the attack on voting rights and extremist policies that criminalize, incarcerate, kill, and deport communities of color and divide the dispossessed.

All Voices: We are here. We are ready. We will break the silence.

Reader 7: "I must remind you that starving a child is violence. Discrimination against working [people] is violence. Ghetto housing is violence. Ignoring medical need is violence. Poverty is violence. Contempt for equality is violence; even a lack of will power to help humanity is a sick and sinister form of violence."—Coretta Scott King

Reader 3: The violence of the war economy and militarism is exacerbated by the structural violence of poverty. True security will only come when communities around the world have access to living-wage jobs, health care, and quality education.

All Voices: We are here. We are ready. We will break the silence.

Reader 5: "We are not faced with two separate crises, one environmental and the other social, but rather one complex crisis which is both social and environmental."—Pope Francis

Reader 6: Climate change, ecological devastation, and pollution are wreaking havoc on our communities, displacing millions of people because of superstorms and man-made disasters. We must protect the environment and the people living in it so that all creation can thrive.

All Voices: We are here. We are ready. We will break the silence.

Reader 7: We are here, we are ready to follow in the footsteps of the prophet Isaiah: If you remove the yoke of oppression, the pointing of the finger, the speaking of evil, if you offer your food to the hungry and satisfy the needs of the afflicted, then your light shall rise in the darkness and your gloom be like the noonday. You shall raise up the foundations of many generations; you shall be called the repairer of the breach, the restorer of streets to live in (Isaiah 58:10–12).

All Voices: As with these sacred texts, we, too, proclaim revival across this land. We sound the alarm and shout WE ARE HERE! It is time to break the silence. It is time for a Poor People's Campaign. It is time for a moral revival.

A PRAYER FOR FREEDOM

A Poem for Freedom Now

This prose poem-as-prayer was created by Rev. Andrew Wilkes, inspired by the frustration of seeing only a fraction of demands met through direct action and lobbying. Wilkes is a pastor and author of multiple books, including

Plenty Good Room, *with over twelve years of experience in public policy, faith-rooted advocacy, and organizing. He is the cofounding, colead pastor of Double Love Experience (DLE), a Brooklyn congregation dedicated to the liberating ministry of Jesus Christ. DLE advances God's love and justice through worship, education, organizing, and radical discipleship.*

I'll take a bit more freedom, please.
Freedom from public policy permeated with the insidious
  incrementalism of "this is the best we could do."

We've all heard that line a million times.
We'll take a bit more freedom, please.

Isn't it for freedom that Christ has set us free?

Human rights aren't breadcrumbs.
And didn't we make the whole loaf?
I'll take a bit more freedom, please.

Bernice Johnson Reagon said it well: "we who believe in freedom
  cannot rest until it comes."

And how might freedom come?

By praying and protesting.
By picketing as an expression of liberation theology.
By pushing back against powers and principalities
Who push down budget cuts and shredded programs to our people.

Freedom, some say, is for the next election, for when the economy
  recovers.

But we dare to differ.
We want the full plate of freedom.
And we're done with saying please.

A POEM TO CONFRONT WHITE CHRISTIAN NATIONALISM

A Poem of Resistance

Sister Ramona Daily Navarro is a member of the Deaconess Community of the Evangelical Lutheran Church of America in Northern Virginia and is an active leader with the Poor People's Campaign: A National Call for Moral Revival, and Freedom Church of the Poor.

White Christian Nationalism
Ain't no new thing
My ancestors endured
White preachers
Dehumanizing them in sermons
Sunday after Sunday
On plantations and in the city
Preachers' mistake:
They read from the B-I-B-L-E
My people heard the word
It took root in the listeners' soul
Who gathered by themselves
In the invisible church of God
Which is indestructible
Souls were freed
We raced to freedom
The truth about ourselves
Is written in Scripture
Whether we are Black and/or gay
Trans and/or poor
This much I know is true.

ORGANIZATIONS

Editors' Note: The following is a list of contemporary movement-related organizations referenced or associated with the rituals and liturgical resources featured in this book. We encourage you to explore these organizations to learn more about their work, and if they are in your area, consider connecting with and supporting their efforts. 🌐

Abahlali baseMojondolo
Adalah Justice Project
American Friends Service Committee
Amnesty International USA
Beloved Community Center of Greensboro
Black Christians for Palestine
Black Youth Project 100
CALEB Venezuela
Center for Constitutional Rights
Center for Earth Ethics
Chaplains on the Harbor
Church of the Common Ground
Coalition of Immokalee Workers
Community Outreach Center at Asbury First United Methodist Church
Council on American-Islamic Relations NY
Deaconess Community of the Evangelical Lutheran Church of America
Domestic Workers United
Donkeysaddle Projects
Double Love Experience

Dream Defenders
Dream Defenders SunDDAy School
Flobots
Freedom Church of the Poor
Freedom Shul of the Poor
Greater Birmingham Ministries
GreenFaith
Highlander Research and Education Center
Hindus for Human Rights
Iglesia del Pueblo
Interfaith Worker Justice
Jewish Voice for Peace
Kairos Center for Religions, Faith, and Social Justice
Kansas Interfaith Action
Labor-Religion Coalition of New York State
Lititz Chooses Love
Maple Street Community Garden
Muslim Justice Initiative
My Sisters' Place
National Coalition for the Homeless
National Health Care for the Homeless Council
National Union of the Homeless
NC Raise Up
Nonviolent Medicaid Army
Open Table Nashville
Peace Poets
People's Institute for Survival and Beyond
Picture the Homeless
Poor People's Campaign: A National Call for Moral Revival
Put People First! PA
Rabbis for Ceasefire
Red Letter Christians
Repairers of the Breach
Restaurant Opportunities Center of NY

Rising Majority
Rivertown Pride Center
Sadhana: Coalition of Progressive Hindus
San Diego Immigrant Rights Consortium
The Open Table KC
The Simple Way
Tía Chucha's Centro Cultural & Bookstore
Union de Vecinos
Union of Southern Service Workers
Unitarian Universalist Refugee and Immigrant Services and Education
United for Respect
United Workers
University of the Poor
US Campaign for Palestinian Rights
Vermont Workers' Center
War Resisters League
Witness Against Torture
Women for Afghan Women

CONTRIBUTORS

Editors' Note: These are the contributors whose work appears in chapters 1 to 5. Short biographical notes about the contributors of resources in chapter 6 appear above those resources.

Adam Thiesen comes from a family of unionized workers and grew from those roots to be a worker, musician, activist, and organizer. He has organized around issues including food insecurity, housing, and workers' rights. He is a leader in the Poor People's Campaign: A National Call for Moral Revival, and currently living in Illinois.

Amy Gopp is the senior pastor at Kent United Church of Christ in Kent, Ohio, and an accomplished author and editor. She coedited *Split Ticket: Independent Faith in a Time of Partisan Politics* and the forthcoming *Help and Hope: Disaster Preparedness and Response Tools for Congregations*. Amy serves on the board of IMA World Health and is a founding member of the We Will Speak Out US campaign to end sexual and gender-based violence.

ana g. lara lópez is the coordinator of Freedom Church of the Poor Care and Engagement for the Kairos Center. Born in Antigua, Guatemala, ana has lived in various places that shaped her worldview. She holds a BA in sociology and anthropology and an MDiv in spiritual care and collective liberation.

Anu Yadav is a critically acclaimed actress, playwright, facilitator, and cultural organizer focused on poor people's organizing, economic justice, and care. She wrote and performed the solo plays *Capers* and *Meena's Dream* and is developing *We the Poor*, a musical.

Arelis Figueroa is the cofounder and lead pastor at La Iglesia Del Pueblo, a PCUSA 1001 New Worshiping Community. With over twenty years of experience as an activist and community organizer, she has worked extensively with marginalized communities, both in the USA and abroad. Arelis also serves at the Dominican Women Development Center and is a member of the New York State Poor People's Campaign. She holds an MDiv from Union Theological Seminary.

Ashley Hufnagel is an organizer, artist, and scholar active in the movement to end poverty since 2006. Originally from New Orleans, she cofounded the Oak Hill Center for Education and Culture in Baltimore and is now the executive director of United Workers. She earned her PhD in American studies in 2021.

Beth Johnson is currently the minister of the Unitarian Church of Hinsdale, having served Palomar Unitarian Universalist Fellowship in California for eighteen years. A minister, activist, and spiritual director grounded in trauma-informed somatic practices, she focuses on embodied, soulful, justice-centered worship and intersectional issues including immigration, environmental justice, and Palestinian liberation.

Cedar Monroe is an activist and interfaith chaplain with over a decade of experience supporting people facing homelessness, incarceration, and addiction. Raised in a poor, rural community, they focus on cross-racial organizing and combating white nationalism. Monroe holds an MDiv from Episcopal Divinity School and is a PhD student at University College Cork.

Charito Calvachi-Mateyko is a restorative justice international consultant, and a passionate promoter of racial justice and the Latinx causes and culture. She was a member of the Delaware Poor People's Campaign: A National Call for Moral Revival and Iglesia del Pueblo. She has had rich and diverse experiences such as being a radio show host, an author, a storyteller, and a Delaware Humanities presenter and facilitator.

Charon Hribar is a song leader, cultural organizer, and social ethicist. She serves as the director of cultural strategies for the Kairos Center and co-director of theomusicology and movement arts for the Poor People's

Campaign: A National Call for Moral Revival. With more than two decades of experience, Dr. Hribar empowers leaders to integrate rituals and arts into organizing efforts.

Christine Lewis is a multidisciplinary performing artist: an actress, poet, musician, organizer, activist, and member of the Domestic Workers United (DWU). From advocating in Albany for a Domestic Workers Bill of Rights to hosting poetry Pop-ups in the Park, Christine amplifies the need for fair labor standards and a decent living wage, while advocating for power and respect for women who live and work in the shadows.

Ciara Taylor is a multimedia artist and cultural strategies organizer at the Kairos Center, focusing on political education and cultural organizing. Cofounder of the Dream Defenders in 2012, she co-created Songs in the Key of Resistance in 2018 to amplify movement music.

Claire Chadwick is a licensed American Baptist pastor and pastoral counselor with Creating Joy Therapy, LLC. She has been involved with the Kairos Center for over fifteen years. Claire is now involved with the Kansas Poor People's Campaign: A National Call for Moral Revival.

Daniel Jones is an educator, organizer, and librarian based in Miami, Florida, and a member of the University of the Poor and the Freedom Shul of the Poor. His research and writing focus on the roots of Jewish traditions of justice in the historical freedom struggles of the ancient Israelites and their meaning for us today.

Harrison Farina is an organizer with Put People First! PA and currently co-coordinates their state-wide Base Building Team. He is also a leader in the Nonviolent Medicaid Army and helped found the PA Homeless Union. He is a Medicaid recipient and committing his life to uniting the poor and dispossessed.

Isaiah Briggs has a MDiv from Harvard Divinity School where he focused on the role of music in social movements and faith communities. His work centers on bringing creative and social development programs to young people dealing with PTSD and complex trauma.

Jacob Butterly is a banjo-playing revolutionary of peace, a coordinator with Put People First! PA, and a theomusicologist with the Pennsylvania Poor People's Campaign.

Jessica Anderson deeply values learning as a site of liberation. She views herself as a student of her elders, ancestors, community, and the divine. She is a graduate of the University of Florida (BA), Georgia State University (MPA), and Howard University (MDiv). At work, she trains an emerging generation of water protectors, activists, and freedom fighters. After work, she takes joy in accompanying young people on their spiritual journeys through youth ministry, as well as offering facilitation and spiritual support to movement kin and causes.

Jessica Williams, a pastor and theological educator, serves as director of ministry education at the Kairos Center, working with Freedom Church of the Poor. With an MDiv, MSW, and PhD, she has pastored churches, led theological programs, and published works on poverty and social justice. She lives in Kansas City.

Joanna Dickson is a leader with the Union of Southern Service Workers. Born and raised in Atlanta, Georgia, she aged out of the foster system at eighteen and became a mother to her amazing son Peyton in 2010. This movement is close to her heart because she too has struggled and witnessed some of the worst injustice in our poor societies. She stands in solidarity.

Jonathan Lykes is a Black, queer artist, activist, and academic dedicated to merging cultural organizing and systemic policy change. As founder and executive director of Liberation House, Jonathan works to teach liberation praxis by pushing the revolutionary edge of transformative movement work. A founding member of BYP100, he curates The Black Joy Experience album, blending Black radical traditions and healing.

Joshua Blaine is a community song leader, Jewish ritualist and storyteller, and cultural organizer with the Jewish Voice for Peace and other movements for justice. He is currently pursuing the path of the Shomeret Shalom, or Practitioner of the Torah of Nonviolence, under the tutelage of Rabbi Lynn Gottlieb.

Julia Willis is a leader in the Nonviolent Medicaid Army based in Wyoming.

Kate Kanelstein is the director of the Vermont Workers' Center and a leader in the Nonviolent Medicaid Army.

Katie Vandersall Thiesen has a master's of science in social administration and an MDiv concentrating in interreligious engagement. She is a daughter, sister, wife, worker, and organizer. Katie is a leader in the Poor People's Campaign: A National Call for Moral Revival, currently living in Illinois.

Katrina Ross Zezza has been coordinating creative content and digital products for over ten years and holds an MDiv from Union Theological Seminary with an interdisciplinary focus in psychology and religion, and theology in the arts.

Kenia Torres-Alcocer is the codirector and organizer with Union de Vecinos and a leader in the Los Angeles Tenants Union. Since 2003, she has organized neighborhood committees in Boyle Heights and Maywood. An undocumented mother of three, she serves on the steering committee of the Poor People's Campaign: A National Call for Moral Revival.

Leonardo Vilchis, trained in liberation theology and a seasoned organizer in Boyle Heights, cofounded Union de Vecinos in 1996 to prevent the demolition of the Pico Aliso public housing projects, securing the right of return for two hundred and fifty families. He also cofounded the LA Tenants Union in 2015 and continues to lead efforts against gentrification and displacement.

Letiah Fraser is an ordained pastor, organizer with the KS Poor People's Campaign, a disability advocate, a hospital chaplain, and identifies as a proud African American woman who lives with cerebral palsy. Rev. Dr. Fraser received her BS in adolescent education with a concentration in English from Nyack College (now Alliance University). She received her MDiv degree from Nazarene Theological Seminary (NTS) in Kansas City. In addition, she received her DMin from NTS with a focus was on disability theology and spiritual formation.

Liz Theoharis is a theologian, pastor, author, and antipoverty activist. She is the executive director of the Kairos Center for Religions, Rights, and Social Justice and co-chair of the Poor People's Campaign: A National Call for Moral Revival. Rev. Dr. Theoharis has been organizing in poor and low-income communities for the past thirty years.

Lu Aya is a cofounder of the Peace Poets, a hip-hop and spoken word crew from The Bronx that has made an indelible mark on the social movements of our times by composing and leading songs sung around the world for justice and liberation. He is a Fordham University graduate with a BA in public health and healing, and designs programs integrating art, human rights, and public health, facilitating community workshops in over thirty countries.

Luis J. Mixcoatl Itztlacuiloh Rodriguez is an acclaimed poet, novelist, journalist, and activist with sixteen books to his name, including the bestselling memoirs *Always Running: La Vida Loca: Gang Days in L.A.* and *It Calls You: An Odyssey Through Love, Addiction, Revolutions, and Healing.* He cofounded several organizations, including Tía Chucha Press and Tía Chucha's Centro Cultural & Bookstore, promoting arts and community in Los Angeles.

Lynn Lewis is an oral historian, educator, and community organizer. She served as executive director of Picture the Homeless for seventeen years, has been an adjunct professor at The New School since 2020, is an adviser to the Housing Justice Oral History Project there, and teaches fieldwork for the oral history MA program at Columbia University. Lynn has been instrumental in initiatives like the East Harlem Community Land Trust and Communities United for Police Reform and is formerly homeless.

Matt Rosing is a coordinator with Put People First! PA, a minister with the Freedom Church of the Poor, a board member of the National Union of the Homeless, and a faith leader with the Poor People's Campaign. He lives in Lancaster, Pennsylvania.

Moses Hernandez McGavin is an organizer with the Nonviolent Medicaid Army and the Freedom Church of the Poor. He is a ministry coordinator with the Church of the Common Ground in Atlanta, Georgia, and is a playwright, cultural worker, and teacher.

Phil Wider has been an organizer and political educator in the American movement to end poverty for over thirty-five years. He currently serves as a coordinator of political education and leadership development with Put People First! PA and the Nonviolent Medicaid Army. He is also a leader of the University of the Poor.

Rebecca Schuchat is a cartoonist and organizer with the Vermont Workers' Center, Nonviolent Medicaid Army, Poor People's Campaign, and Freedom Shul of the Poor. Raised Jewish in the Bay Area, her commitment to *Tikkun Olam* (healing the world) inspires her to create political and socially engaged art that investigates existing power structures and dreams of a world where power is in the hands of the people.

Sarah Weintraub is a dedicated mother and organizer who joined the movement for health care rights in 2008 through the Vermont Workers' Center. Now based in Milwaukee, she organizes with the Nonviolent Medicaid Army and serves as a tri-chair of the Wisconsin Poor People's Campaign.

Savina Martin, a lifelong organizer and an army veteran from Massachusetts, has organized around issues impacting homeless families, women, and veterans in Boston and San Diego. Dr. Martin is active in the University of the Poor's Homeless Union History Project and the Massachusetts Poor People's Campaign, and serves as a minister at the Freedom Church of the Poor.

Stephen Brackett (Brer Rabbit) and **Jamie Laurie** (Jonny 5) are childhood friends and emcees with the Colorado-based band, Flobots. They create and perform music as a resource for social movements. In 2014 they cofounded the NOENEMIES initiative, convening musicians, organizers, and community members to develop musical tactics for social movements. They are also cofounders of Youth on Record, a Denver organization empowering at-risk youth through music programs and a state-of-the-art Youth Media Studio. In addition to Flobots, they continue to pursue work that bridges the music, grassroots movements, and education sectors. Laurie is director of community engagement at Project Worthmore, a nonprofit organization serving refugees and immigrants. Brackett is the executive director at Foundation Music School.

Tammy Rosing is a tri-chair of the Pennsylvania Poor People's Campaign: National Call for Moral Revival and a coordinator with Put People First! PA and the National Union of the Homeless.

Tim Seitz Brown is an Evangelical Lutheran Church in America (ELCA) pastor. Since 1987, he has served congregations in Easton, Ephrata, Thomasville, Biglerville, Lancaster, and Landisville, Pennsylvania. As an ELCA Global Mission volunteer, he has also taught at a high school in Tanzania. Currently, he is active as a faith leader in the Pennsylvania Poor People's Campaign: A National Call for Moral Revival and March on Harrisburg.

Tonny Algood has worked as a union organizer in Mississippi and Alabama and served as a local pastor for the United Methodist Inner City Mission, the National Union of the Homeless, and the Freedom Church of the Poor.

Trini Tlazohteotl Rodriguez is cofounder and former executive director of Tía Chucha's, a cultural center and bookstore that transforms communities through ancestral knowledge, literacy, and the arts. Rodriguez is a former teacher, interpreter, and editor who now works for personal and collective healing in harmony with systemic social change.

Vanessa Cardinale is the associate director of the Center for Transformational Leadership, with twenty years of experience in community organizing and church leadership in the United States and Latin America. She has served as an associate pastor in Brooklyn and lead pastor in Massachusetts, focusing on cross-cultural bridge building, partnerships, immersion experiences, and advocacy across diverse communities.

William Burnett joined Picture the Homeless (PTH) as a member in 2004 and was instrumental in leading the Housing and Potters Field campaigns. He was also a board member of PTH.

PERMISSIONS

CHAPTER 1

Passover Seder: The Ritual © 2025 Freedom Shul; We Get There Together © 2025 Joshua Blaine; Communion: The Ritual excerpted from *The United Methodist Hymnal* © 1992 The United Methodist Publishing House. Used by permission. All rights reserved; Stations of the Cross © 2025 Cedar Monroe; Stations of the Cross images © 2025 Katrina Ross Zezza; Dia de los Muertos © 2025 ana g. lara lópez, Arelis Figueroa, and Charito Calvachi-Mateyko; Longest Night of the Year © 2025 Timothy Seitz Brown

CHAPTER 2

Footwashing: The Prayers © 2025 Moses Hernandez McGavin; Gathering in the Garden: The Prayer/Poem (Coming Back to The Garden Post Covid 19/A Song for Denise Williams) © 2025 Christine Lewis; An Indigenous Prayer of Gratitude and Reflection © 2025 Trini Tlazohteotl Rodriguez and Luis J. Mixcoatl Itztlacuiloh Rodriguez; Healthcare Vigil: The Litany © 2025 Letiah Fraser and Claire Chadwick

CHAPTER 3

The Potter's Field Liturgy © 2025 Amy Gopp; Prayer of Response © 2025 William Burnett; "We Remember You": The Rap © 2025 Jamie Laurie; A Eulogy: The Ritual © 2025 Ashley Hufnagel

CHAPTER 4

Her Name Is Poverty ©2025 Joanna Dickson; Ceasefire Pray-In ©2025 Jessica Anderson; A Project of Survival: Prayer © 2025 Katie Vandersall Thiesen; 1-2-3 Lift Up: A Song © 2025 Adam Thiesen; Prayer for Migrant Justice: The Poem © 2025 Beth Johnson; Vigil for the Detained: The Song © 2025 The Peace Poets

CHAPTER 5

Litany for a Celebration © 2025 Vanessa Cardinale and Jessica Williams; Prayer for a Movement Anniversary: The Litany © 2025 Savina Martin; Chant of the Ancestors © 2025 Jonathan Lykes; Song of Belonging for Community Organizing: The Story: adapted from Anu Yadu, "Being Together: The Revolutionary Love of a Poor People's Movement" in *We Are Civic Media* copyright © 2025 by Northwestern University. Published 2025 by Northwestern University Press. All rights reserved. Used with permission; We Belong Together: The Song © 2025 Anu Yadav

CHAPTER 6

An Interfaith Litany for Building Power © 2025 Derrick McQueen; Communion Liturgy © 2025 Adam Barnes and Arelis Figueroa; Covid-19 Memorial: An Interfaith Litany for Healing and Justice © 2025 Jessica Williams; A Bilingual Immigrant Creed © 2025 Iglesia del Pueblo; A Prayer for Justice and Inclusion © 2025 Chris Wylie; Earth Liturgy © 2025 Chelsea MacMillan; Poem for a Hunger Strike © 2025 Azmera Hammouri-Davis; A Ramadan Ritual © 2025 Jamel Coy Hudson; Invocation for the Future © 2025 Ari Douglas; A Prayer for Pentecost © 2025 Tim Shenk; Benediction for Homeless Persons' Memorial Day © 2025 Lindsey Krinks; A Palm Sunday Litany © 2025 Kelly Smith; Imposition of the Ashes © 2025 Patrick Dupont; Litany of Remembrance © 2025 Alex Zane; Liturgy for the Earth © 2025 Karenna Gore; A Poem in the Wake of Police Violence © 2025 Tony Eskridge; Power of Love © 2025 Steff Reed; May This Body Be a Bridge © 2025 Te Martin; Mothers and Children for Peace © 2025 Holly Haile Thompson; A Shiva Prayer © 2025 Sunita Viswanath; A Prayer of Commitment to Social Justice © 2025 Carolyn Foster; A Prayer for Black Women and Girls © 2025 Kym McNair; A Prayer for Diwali © 2025 Shailly Gupta Barnes; A Prayer for a Local Council Meeting © 2025 Lindsey Krinks; A Prayer for Black August © 2025 Wesley Morris; A Prayer for Healing © 2025 Shane Claiborne; A Revolutionary Advent Wreath © 2025 Becca Forsyth; A Grounding Meditation © 2025 Nubia Chong; A Poem for Freedom Now © 2025 Andrew Wilkes; A Poem of Resistance © 2025 Ramona Daily Navarro

NOTES

INTRODUCTION

xi ***FCOP gets its name:*** Martin Luther King, Jr., "Nonviolence and Social Change," in *The Trumpet of Conscience* (Harper & Row, 1968), 66–67.

xiv ***"the arc of the moral universe is long":*** Martin Luther King, Jr., "Remaining Awake Through a Great Revolution," sermon at the National Cathedral, March 31, 1968, in A *Testament of Hope: The Essential Writings and Speeches of Martin Luther King, Jr.*, ed. James M. Washington (HarperOne, 1991), 277.

xv ***In 1964, on a trip to Arizona State:*** Martin Luther King Jr., "Religious Witness for Human Dignity," (speech, Goodwin Stadium, Arizona State University, Tempe, AZ, June 3, 1964).

CHAPTER 1: REMEMBRANCE

4 ***the story reminds us that a "mixed multitude" rallied alongside them:*** Daniel Jones, "A Mixed Multitude," in *We Cry Justice: Reading the Bible with the Poor People's Campaign*, ed. Liz Theoharis (Broadleaf Books, 2021).

7 ***The Freedom Shul of the Poor materials capture this sentiment:*** Freedom Shul of the Poor, *Haggadah 2024*, https://kairoscenter.org/resources_cpt/passover-haggadah-2024/.

8 ***This midrash tells the story of leadership:*** To read more on the leadership of Nachshon and the importance of leadership by poor and dispossessed people who have nothing to lose when behind them is only death and in front of them the hope of freedom, see Daniel Jones, "The Biblical Nachshon and the Poor People's Campaign," *Tikkun*, April 16, 2020, https://www.tikkun.org/the-biblical-nachshon-poor-peoples-campaign/.

10 ***the Supreme Court will hear the case of Grants Pass v. Johnson:*** On June 28, 2024, the Supreme Court of the United States ruled that cities can punish unhoused people for sleeping outside even when they have nowhere to go. This decision has set off a wave of arrests, fines, and

demolition of homeless encampments in towns and cities across the country.

18 ***according to writer and organizer Aaron Scott:*** Aaron Scott, "Holy Temperance in a Revolutionary Moment," *Updates* (blog), Kairos Center for Religions, Rights, and Social Justice, November 18, 2020, https://kairoscenter.org/holy-temperance-revolutionary-moment/.

18 ***"God takes sides":*** Cedar Monroe in *America Will Be*, episode 3, "Spirit of Struggle," Poor People's Campaign video, February 26, 2018, video, 7:40, https://youtu.be/qRmM3zSwZk4?si=uC68ghMmnYUwlCBH.

19 ***In Grays Harbor, we walk our own Way of the Cross:*** Kairos Center, "Stations of the Cross from Grays Harbor County," *Updates* (blog), Kairos Center for Religions, Rights, and Social Justice, March 26, 2016, https://kairoscenter.org/stations-cross-grays-harbor-county/.

35 ***estimates suggesting that between eight million and eleven million people are homeless:*** Poor People's Campaign: A National Call for Moral Revival, *Housing Fact Sheet*, June 4, 2020, https://www.poorpeoplescampaign.org/resource/housing-fact-sheet/.

CHAPTER 2: HEALING AND TRANSFORMATION

39 ***Faya Rose Touré's song:*** "I'm Gonna Lift My Sister Up," by Faya Rose Touré (unpublished song).

40 ***Teresa Mateus and Vahisha Hasan offer a compelling answer:*** Teresa Mateus and Vahisha Hasan, "Healing Sustains Our Organizing," in *Building Up a New World: Congregational Organizing for Transformative Impact*, ed. Anne Dunlap and Vahisha Hasan (Pilgrim Press, 2023), 124.

48 ***Here are a couple of broad prompts to get you started:*** These prompts were written by Moses Hernandez McGavin.

CHAPTER 3: MOURNING

63 ***normalizes the death of two hundred and fifty thousand people every year due to poverty:*** Poor People's Campaign: A National Call for Moral Revival, *National Fact Sheet*, May 2023, https://www.poorpeoplescampaign.org/wp-content/uploads/2023/06/2023-National-Fact-Sheet-Template_6-4-8.5-%C3%97-11-in-updated.pdf.

65 ***Over ten million people live without housing:*** Poor People's Campaign: A National Call for Moral Revival, *Housing Fact Sheet*, June 4, 2020, https://www.poorpeoplescampaign.org/resource/housing-fact-sheet/.

68 ***"In terms of the homeless community, we've got to remember that it is a community":*** The Picture the Homeless Oral History Project, *The*

Potter's Field Campaign, https://housingjusticeoralhistory.org/projects/picture-the-homeless-1.

68 ***all documented in the MDiv thesis of Rev. Amy Gopp:*** Amy Gopp, "Ritualizing with the Poor: The Potter's Field Memorial Service," *Liturgy* 23, no. 1 (December 2007): 15–19, doi:10.1080/04580630701673232.

69 ***"These are people who in life were disrespected, abused, pushed aside":*** Eileen Markey, "Homeless, Nameless—and Honored," *City Limits*, March 25, 2010, https://citylimits.org/2010/03/25/homeless-nameless-and-honored/.

70 ***Dawn Quinones reminded those gathered:*** *"With All Due Respect": A Memorial Service for Those Buried at Potter's Field* (New York: Union Theological Seminary, March 23, 2005), https://kairoscenter.org/wp-content/uploads/2014/10/Gopp_PTH_Potters_Field_Liturgy.pdf.

73 ***Call to Worship from Matthew:*** **HMO**—Health Maintenance Organization; **MTA**—Metropolitan Transportation Authority in the New York City metropolitan area; **NYPD**—New York Police Department.

80 ***a local television reporter asked if now was the "right time":*** United Workers and National Economic and Social Rights Initiative, *Hidden In Plain Sight: Workers at Baltimore's Inner Harbor and the Struggle for Fair Development*, (Spring 2011), v, https://dignityandrights.org/wp-content/uploads/2019/11/Hidden_in_Plain_Sight_Report_compressed_0.pdf.

80 ***she was a Poverty Scholar:*** The Poverty Scholars Program trained hundreds of diverse, low-income leaders from more than two hundred community organizations and religious congregations. The Poverty Scholars Program works to develop a core of sophisticated leaders from communities across the country and around the world who can meet the strategic demands of their local struggles and play their leadership roles toward building the broader movement to end poverty.

81 ***more than two hundred and fifty thousand people:*** Poor People's Campaign: A National Call for Moral Revival, *2023 National Fact Sheet*, June 16, 2023, https://www.poorpeoplescampaign.org/resource/2023-national-fact-sheet/.

83 ***Springfield Hospital, the site of Maryland's Potter's Field:*** Springfield Hospital is the site of Maryland's Potter's field, a mass grave for the unidentified and "unclaimed" cremains of those impoverished Marylanders who were too poor to afford a funeral. According to Maryland law, a family has seventy-two hours to claim their relative's body and provide for their funerary services. If they cannot afford to claim their loved one, the body is taken by the State Anatomy Board and sold whole or in parts as a cadaver for medical research. Their final resting spot is

a mass grave at Springfield Hospital, where a single anonymous plaque marks their contribution to science but makes no mention of the reality that so many did not consent, did not have a choice.

85 ***a Pennsylvania Insurance Department hearing:*** PPF-PA had fought for and won this 2016 hearing that was the first hearing on rising insurance rates since the adoption of the Affordable Care Act.

CHAPTER 4: TAKING ACTION TOGETHER

94 ***"The dispossessed of this nation":*** .Martin Luther King Jr., "Nonviolence and Social Change," in *The Trumpet of Conscience* (Harper & Row, 1968), 66–67.

98 ***"There are forty million poor people here":*** Martin Luther King Jr., "Where Do We Go From Here?": SCLC Presidential Address, August 16, 1967, Atlanta, Georgia, transcript, https://kinginstitute.stanford.edu/where-do-we-go-here.

116 ***"Bearing witness in front of MCC":*** Aviva Stahl, "Why Are Queer Activists and Muslim Scholars Holding Vigils Outside a Manhattan Prison?" *Nation*, May 30, 2014, https://www.thenation.com/article/archive/why-are-queer-activists-and-muslim-scholars-holding-vigils-outside-manhattan-prison/.

CHAPTER 5: CELEBRATION

121 ***"Power for poor people":*** *King: A Filmed. . . Record Montgomery to Memphis*, directed by Sidney Lumet and Joseph L. Mankiewicz, 1970.

125 ***"There are forty million poor people here":*** Martin Luther King Jr., "Where Do We Go From Here?": SCLC Presidential Address, August 16, 1967, Atlanta, Georgia, transcript, https://kinginstitute.stanford.edu/where-do-we-go-here.

128 ***Dr. Martin explained:*** Savina Martin, " 'Seize the moment!'—an Interview with Savina Martin," interview by Erica Williams, *Kairos Center for Religions, Rights, and Social Justice*, March 1, 2016, https://kairoscenter.org/seize-the-moment-interview-with-savina-martin/.

128 ***"It's my responsibility and accountability to do something":*** Martin, "Seize the Moment" by Erica Williams.

131 ***"There are millions of poor people in this country":*** Martin Luther King Jr., "Nonviolence and Social Change," in *The Trumpet of Conscience* (Harper & Row, 1968), 66–67.

132 ***the formation of Black Youth Project 100:*** "Songs and Chants were taught to BYP100 by Jazz Hudson & Tiara Phalon at the first BYP100

Beyond November Convening in Chicago on July 12–14, 2013, which was organized by Dr. Cathy Cohen. In this moment the BYP100 holistic energy culture was formed, as we held hands, 100 Black youth strong, and wept together as we heard the live George Zimmerman verdict. We were broken, but we started to heal, and we started to do the base building work necessary to bring into fruition what we spoke into existence during that very first meeting in Chicago. 'We are here to launch our generation's freedom movement. To ensure that the government immediately meets the interest of the poor.' "—Black Youth Project 100, *Black Joy Experience Resource Guide* (2017), PDF. 🌐

134 ***Jonathan Lykes created a polyrhythmic exercise:*** The Black Joy Experience Resource Guide 🌐

136 ***a play based on their experiences:*** Ana Yadav's play *Capers* is a one-woman show based on the stories of families at DC's Arthur Capper/Carrollsburg public housing project and their protests against the government-funded demolition of their neighborhood.

137 ***Dr. King's understanding of agape love:*** Martin Luther King Jr., "An Experiment with Love," in *A Testament of Hope: The Essential Writings of Martin Luther King, Jr.*, ed. James Melvin Washington (Harper & Row, 1986), 19.

CHAPTER 6: LITURGIES OF THE PEOPLE

146 ***it draws on a variety of Communion liturgies:*** Katherine Hawker, "Liturgy Outside," *Easter Sunday*; Cláudio Carvalhaes, *Liturgies from Below: Praying with People at the Ends of the World* (Abingdon Press, 2020); *Liturgy for Presbytery Celebrations of the Lord's Supper in the Book of Common Worship* (Westminster John Knox Press, 1993).

179 ***Portions of this liturgy are adapted:*** "A Service of Worship for Ash Wednesday," Discipleship Ministries: The United Methodist Church, published November 10, 2014, https://www.umcdiscipleship.org/resources/a-service-of-worship-for-ash-wednesday.

194 ***honors all Black women and girls who have endured violence and control:*** See Danielle L. McGuire, *At the Dark End of the Street: Black Women, Rape, and Resistance—a New History of the Civil Rights Movement from Rosa Parks to the Rise of Black Power* (Alfred A. Knopf, 2010).

206 ***How to create a virtual altar:*** Online participants can participate in creating a virtual altar through an online tool like Google Jamboard (an interactive digital whiteboard where congregants can "jam," or draw, create, or add text to create a collective visualization).